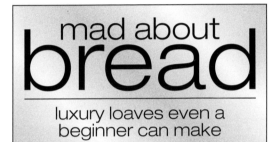

mad about
bread

luxury loaves even a
beginner can make

mad about bread
luxury loaves even a beginner can make

diana bonaparte

foulsham
LONDON • NEW YORK • TORONTO • SYDNEY

foulsham

The Publishing House, Bennetts Close, Cippenham,
Slough, Berkshire, SL1 5AP, England

ISBN 0-572-03049-5

Photographs by Roger and Diana Bonaparte

A CIP record for this book is available from the British Library

Acknowledgements
First, to Karen Rowberry, Frank Kingdom and David Williams, who suggested I
write a book in the first place – thank you for all your help and support.

A big thank you to my husband Roger, my son Corin, my Doberman Piper and
the rest of my family – who put up with lots of questions every time they took a
bite of something new and often had to wait until I'd taken photos before they
could eat (especially Piper)!

Another equally big thank you to Samantha and Keith Merrifield and Gill Owen
and family for your endless support and love. My thanks to Dot and Howard
Greville and David and Hilary Hall.

Thank you to everyone at Foulsham.

Finally, thank you to my classmates and everyone in the Bakery Department at
Plymouth College of Further Education, to everyone at Stadtische Berufsschule
fur das Backer-und Konditorendhandwerk Munchen, and everyone at Rischart
Bakery in Munich.

Printed in Malaysia

Contents

Introduction	7
Before you start	9
Making the dough	12
Moulding the dough into a head	14
Tips on rising and resting	15
Moulding round	16
Rolling out rounds	18
Rolling out sausages	20
Rolling out a rectangle	21
Chopping ingredients into the bread dough	23
Using a bread machine	24
Baking your loaves	26
Notes on the recipes	26
Perfect loaves	27
Sandwich loaves	43
Fancy loaves	57
Rolls and buns	67
Filled rolls and buns	83
Pizza	111
Flat breads	121
Fancy bakes	133
Muffins	147
Bibliography	165
Index	166

Introduction

I'm just mad about bread and I want you to experience how much fun making bread can be and how good it can taste! To start with, forget any unnecessary pressure that your home baking should look like supermarket products, which are strictly regulated by size, weight, customer demand and cost.

Home baking doesn't need to address any of these issues; baking at home is about the flavours and textures you like at a cost that suits you. Once you are familiar with handling and working with dough, your only limits are your imagination.

I love making and eating something I cannot buy in a shop. I often use freeform shapes in this book because, though I maintain evenly sized portions as this is essential to ensure each piece will bake properly, I enjoy individuality. We are not going to produce a sheet of rolls to adorn a bakery window, where they must all be identical to avoid customers choosing one roll over another. We are going to bake some wonderful things to eat, which appeal to the eye and the imagination. The breads in this book rely less on your skill at producing identical specimens and more on your enthusiasm to get involved with flavour, texture and variety.

I have written this book so that everyone can make fantastic bread and get good results every time. To achieve that, you do need to weigh, measure and follow the instructions carefully, but I've included both general principles so you understand the processes and techniques, and specific instructions for every recipe so there's no reason why you should go wrong.

I have written the instructions for the recipes to help free you from the two main uncertainties of working with yeast: time and temperature. I cannot control how warm your kitchen is or your oven's temperament, but I have tried to take away some of the time and temperature variables by using a free-standing mixer with a dough hook and a temperature probe to measure the temperature of the liquids added to the dough (see page 12). You can hand mix your dough if you prefer but, if you are inexperienced, it can be very difficult to know if you have kneaded the dough enough – the results of 5 minutes' kneading can be very different from person to person.

Where appropriate, I have also included instructions on how to adapt the recipes for use with a breadmaker. Different machines have slightly different characteristics, so you will need to experiment a bit with your own machine, but I'm sure you'll soon get the hang of it and get excellent results.

I have also chosen to use easy-blend dried yeast (sometimes called 'fast-action' or 'rapid-rise') rather than fresh yeast. Fresh yeast is often difficult to find and it may not always be at its best. With sachets of easy-blend dried yeast (6 or 7 g depending on the brand), you will know that the yeast is in good condition and that you have the correct amount.

I truly enjoyed writing the book. The more I thought about flavours and textures, the more new ideas and variations came to me. I hope this book will open your mind to the endless possibilities of baking at home. I also hope that, through the experience of reproducing the recipes in this book, you will gain in confidence and discover what fun baking is.

Before you start

Before you start baking, these basic tips and suggestions will help give you the background information you need. I've broken them all down into points so that they will be easy to refer to when you want to come back and find a particular piece of information. In any event, nearly all the recipes contain all the details you need to complete the loaf.

Enjoy!

First off, baking is not a chore or a test. It doesn't make you mumsy, grannyish or a wimp! You bake to make delicious things to eat – it's as simple as that. You can make the whole thing even more fun by putting on the radio or your favourite CD and singing, whistling, humming or dancing along – whatever you feel like as you bake or wash up. I don't go out dancing and you'd never hear me sing – I'm too self-conscious – but in my kitchen it's a different story...

Take your time: Bake when you feel like it and don't rush. In fact you can't rush bread; it has a very relaxed take on life and moves along in its own time! Be patient when you are mixing dough or waiting for it to rise. Give yourself time to learn and get a feel for the dough and the look of a batter. What you make at first may not be perfectly shaped but will usually be tasty and the next time you try it will be easier and more familiar.

Get your hands messy: To bake successfully, you do need to accept that your hands will get messy and there will be washing up. I find it's best to wash up as you go; not only does it make it easier in the long run, but it also washes your hands at the same time.

Read the recipe through first: Do read the recipe all the way through before you start and make sure you have enough time, the ingredients and the correct tins (pans) and tools needed. I find it easiest to get everything ready first – it saves rooting around in cupboards or drawers with mucky fingers!

Ingredients

Throughout the book, I have primarily used ordinary supermarket products. There are just a very few items that may be stocked only by a large supermarket or a health food store, such as cornmeal (polenta or maize meal) and rye flour. Once you get the bread-baking bug, you'll find loads of other fascinating ingredients in health food stores that you can try: different flours, huge rolled oats, exotic dried fruits and nuts. I love to use the spicy kick of seaweed peanuts; these are peanuts with a crunchy pink, green, orange or tan coating with seaweed flecks. So do go and have a good browse!

Baking powder and bicarbonate of soda (baking soda): Always use a proper measuring spoon where spoon measures are given, and scrape the excess off the top of the spoon with a knife for a level measure. You must measure accurately or the results will be disappointing.

Black pepper: This is always freshly ground from the pepper mill (though I do use ready-ground white pepper sometimes).

Butter: I use butter rather than margarine, and salted unless unsalted (sweet) is stated in the recipe.

Chocolate: I always use chocolate with 70% cocoa solids in a dough or batter. I do sometimes use very good plain (semi-sweet) chocolate for fillings but you can use either according to your own taste.

Dried fruit: The pre-soaked, ready-to-eat variety.

Eggs: I've based the recipes on medium eggs weighing 50 g/1¾ oz out of their shells. Try to bring them to room temperature before you add them to a bread dough.

Flour: I have used both branded and store-brand strong white bread flour, wholemeal bread flour and plain (all-purpose) flour.

Jams (conserves) and marmalades: Buy the best quality you can or make your own – it is definitely worth the effort as the flavour is much fruitier!

Oils: I generally use vegetable or sunflower oil but you can use any oil that doesn't have a strong flavour. I use extra virgin olive oil when stated in the recipe.

Salt: I prefer finely ground sea salt.

Sugar: I usually use muscovado sugars in my recipes as I love the flavour. Otherwise, I use golden caster (superfine) and golden granulated sugar.

Vanilla essence (extract): I pay the money and buy the good stuff – it's worth it. I also use fresh vanilla pods. After I've split them and used the seeds, I put the empty pod in an airtight container filled with golden caster (superfine) sugar, thus making vanilla sugar. Just keep topping up pods and sugar and you will have a continuous supply.

Yeast: All the recipes that have yeast use the easy-blend (sometimes called 'fast-action' or 'rapid rise') dried variety in sachets.

Equipment

As I mentioned, I like to use a free-standing mixer with a dough hook. You'll obviously need some baking tins (pans) and baking (cookie) sheets but you can certainly start with just your usual kitchen equipment, even if you decide to treat yourself to some new equipment later on.

I recommend you buy a digital scale if you don't already have one.

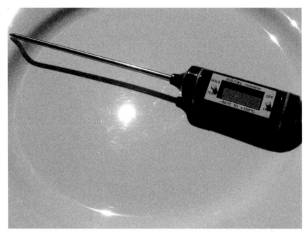

For perfect results, I also use a temperature probe (sometimes called a digital thermometer) to measure liquid temperatures accurately (see Adding the Liquid, page 12).

I also find a rigid metal pastry scraper with a handle is invaluable when it comes to portioning your dough or chopping in ingredients. A small, rounded, rigid plastic one is fine if you already have one but they tend to bend, so, if you bake regularly, you may want to put a metal scraper on your Christmas list.

A really good long serrated bread knife is also a good idea as some of the bread shapes can be difficult to cut with a shorter bread knife.

Be accurate

For best results, it is important that you are accurate with your weights and measurements, but that is easy as long as you follow the instructions in the recipes. Almost all the ingredients in the book are weighed – liquid and dry alike – and I always use grams because it's so much easier. (In the baking industry, liquids aren't measured using a measuring cups or jugs, they are weighed.) Most importantly, this is the most accurate method, but it also quicker and there is less washing up. For very small amounts (below 5 g), I do use measuring spoons.

My method using a digital scale is to place the bowl on top and set the reading to zero. I weigh the first ingredient, leave it in the bowl and reset the reading to zero, weigh another ingredient and reset to zero again. And so on.

I also find I get the best results when dividing dough into portions if I weigh out each portion, rather than just dividing the dough roughly into even-sized pieces. If there is any left over, it's then more accurate to share it out evenly between the portions

Getting used to the method

Don't be daunted if the methods look long. I have tried to write the instructions so that an absolute beginner can make any bread or muffin in the book. All that's involved in most of the bread recipes is: mixing for 2 minutes and 10 minutes, rising, portioning, resting, shaping, rising and baking.

Make it yours

This is your cookbook, so do write notes to yourself about substitutions you make or anything else that will be helpful. I always write the date next to a new recipe I'm trying and whether or not I liked it, so my cookbooks all have 'yucky', 'yummy', 'to die for' or some variation (though you won't need that first comment for this book!). I also write in if the meal was for a special occasion or what I thought went well with the recipe. It's nice to see your anniversary or birthday meal from five years ago as you flick through a cookbook. Sometimes, if something was really special or came out particularly well or if there wasn't a picture in the cookbook, I take a photo and stick that in as well.

Making the dough

Now you are ready to start! The next few sections will take you step by step through the principles of breadmaking, including lots of useful hints and tips from the professionals. It is a good idea to read through these principles first, then you will find it much easier to follow the recipes when you start making your bread.

Checking your mixer speeds

I mix my doughs in a free-standing mixer using a dough hook. My mixer has speeds 1–10, but for making bread I use only speed 1 for the initial mixing and speed 2 for the 10-minute mix. There is no need to use a high speed to knead the dough. Do check with your manufacturer's instructions, especially about the total flour weight your machine can handle.

Measuring out your dry ingredients

As I mentioned, I use a digital scale (see page 11). Place the bowl from your mixer on the scale and set the reading to zero. Weigh the first ingredient, leave it in the bowl and reset to zero, then continue adding and weighing ingredients and resetting in this way. Place all the dry ingredients in your mixing bowl in the order listed in the recipe, starting with the flour and working through the remaining dry ingredients. Never put salt or sugar directly on your yeast as both of these can kill it. Keep that yeast well away from them!

If you are very new to baking, you can tick off the ingredients next to the recipe lightly in pencil as you add them. It's not silly, it helps!

Adding the liquid

Once you have added all the dry ingredients, you are ready to add the liquids. Melted butter, oils, syrups and so on can be added to the dough as they are but water, yoghurt, milk, ginger beer or other liquids should be brought to 36˚C/97˚F. For perfect results, I use a temperature probe, which is ideal. If you don't

have one, this is just about blood heat, so if you put in a clean finger it should feel neither hot nor cold.

Add all the liquid ingredients to the bowl, measuring them in the same way as the dry ingredients, then finally add the water.

Checking the texture

The first mixing allows you to check the texture of the dough, as different flours and even room temperatures can affect the finished results. You are aiming for a smooth dough that spins around in a ball without smearing on the bottom of the bowl. To achieve this, you may have to add a little more water or flour, although you should be only 15–45 ml/

Kneading the dough

When I'm happy with the texture, I switch the mixer up to the next speed and mix for 10 minutes until the dough is stretchy, smooth and soft (my husband says the dough 'feels like a breast'!). During the 10-minute mixing time, the dough is kneaded and the gluten in the bread flour is developed so it will rise and spring in the oven; so don't cheat on the kneading!

Making adjustments

During the 10-minute mix, you may still need to make water or flour adjustments to the dough to maintain the correct texture and stop the dough smearing on the bottom of your bowl. Enriched doughs (those with eggs, cream or extra butter) often need top-ups of flour.

1–3 tbsp of either water or flour away from the correct texture.

I give an initial 2-minute mixing on the slowest setting of the mixer. After 1 minute I check the texture of the dough and if it looks dry I add 15 g/ ½ oz of warm water and watch it mix in thoroughly to see that the dough is the correct texture. If the dough is still looking lumpy and stiff, I add another 15 g/½ oz of warm water. On the other hand, if the dough is really wet, I add 15 g/½ oz of flour, again checking the dough texture and a further couple of spoonfuls, one at a time, if necessary.

You don't have to get the texture perfect in just 2 minutes; this is a guide. Do turn the machine off at any time and give the dough a squeeze to check its texture. At this stage you want it to be beginning to feel smooth, pliable and not sticky.

You can turn off the mixer at any stage to check the dough's texture – it is important, especially when mixing in a machine, to feel the dough and see how it's coming along.

Mixing by hand

Mixing by hand varies so much from person to person that it's difficult to specify the right length of time for kneading. You should start by kneading for double the specified machine time, checking the consistency of the dough as you work. You may need to carry on for longer than this to achieve the smooth, stretchy and soft dough you need.

Moulding the dough into a head

Once you have mixed and kneaded the dough for the recipe to the correct consistency, you need to shape the dough into a 'head' to help the dough rise properly and give it strength. This is a professional technique that is not easy to explain, but with a bit of practice you'll soon get the idea.

All that matters is that you form the dough into a smooth tight ball; you will see a spiral on the base of your rounded dough that is most obvious on small portions. This is the head. Don't worry if you don't have perfectly smooth moulding to begin with; just work with the dough and remember it will rise even if it's in a heap! Obviously, you can use your other hand, but be consistent in reversing left and right in the instructions.

Knocking back the dough

Knocking back is when you push all the air out of the dough, knead it gently a few times, then let the dough rise again. You use the same moulding technique after knocking the dough back to re-shape it into a head.

Step by step moulding into a head

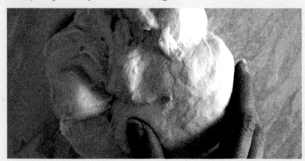

1 Knead the dough on your work surface until you have a nice compact ball. Place your right hand up against and slightly on top on the right-hand side of the dough with your little finger on the work surface. If the dough is a bit sticky you may need to scatter it with flour at the kneading stage – but not during the moulding because it would just make the dough slip.

2 With continuous downward pressure and keeping your fingers cupped around the dough, push the dough forwards slightly, about 7.5 cm/3 in and then curl the dough around until your hand almost reaches the left side of the dough.

3 Keeping the same downward pressure, scoop the dough back towards you about the same distance you pushed it forward. You will see the top of the dough becoming smoother.

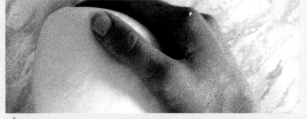

4 Then shift your hand to the starting position again and repeat the whole process in nice, smooth motions until you have a smooth, round head.

Tips on rising and resting

You will need to leave your dough to rest and rise at various stages of the process. Keep portions of dough you are not working with covered with clingfilm (plastic wrap), or a clean plastic grocery bag, then a tea towel (dish cloth). You don't want the air to dry out the surface and form a crust or skin, which would inhibit rising before and during baking.

Rising

You will leave the dough to rise either in the mixing bowl or after it has been shaped. It is equally important to keep the dough covered while it is rising and, again, you can use clingfilm, or a plastic bag, and a tea towel (the tea towel on top helps to keep the dough just that bit warmer. You don't need to leave the dough in a hot spot to rise. I simply leave mine in the kitchen. In a cooler place, though, it will take a little longer to rise.

While the dough is rising, make sure it is on a surface that won't be bumped or exposed to sudden changes in temperature, both of which could make it collapse. Also, move sheets and tins (pans) of rising or risen loaves or rolls gently – don't bash them about or slam the oven door.

Where I have given instructions to allow the dough to rise for a certain length of time or until doubled in size but it doesn't seem to have managed to double, you should need to leave it for only a further 15–30 minutes.

Resting and relaxing

Once you have kneaded or shaped the dough, you are often told to leave it to rest or relax for a short time before finishing or baking. This makes the dough easier to shape or roll out. Simply cover it as before and leave it in the kitchen.

Solving problems

If your dough has over-risen during the initial rising – perhaps formed a great air bubble and burst or it looks like its going to burst – just knock it back, mould it into a head (see page 14), cover and leave to rise again. It will come up quicker this time so keep an eye on it.

If you have already portioned and shaped the dough into rolls or loaves and they have over-risen, you can usually solve the problem quite easily. In most cases, you can just knock back the dough, mould it into a head or the individual portions, mould it round (see pages 16–17), cover and allow to rest for 10–20 minutes. Then simply reshape the dough and allow it to rise again before baking. Again, the dough will come up quicker.

The only exception would be a filled loaf, for example Hot Dog Sandwich Loaf (see page 46), which could be rescued if it had over-risen during the initial rising but not after it had been filled.

If you have left your dough an extra half an hour and it still hasn't risen, think back on the recipe.
- Did you add everything – especially the yeast?
- Was the water too hot or too cold?
- Did you mix the dough for long enough?
- Has the rising dough been bumped or exposed to sudden temperature change?

If you have done everything correctly, then just give the dough more time. Some days it will move more slowly than on others.

Moulding round

The next stage is to divide the dough into portions, as dictated by the recipe, so you'll have lots of little heaps of dough. You then need to form these portions into smooth, round balls of dough. This 'moulding round', as it is called, helps the dough to rise well and gives the maximum amount of 'spring' in the oven.

It is important to learn this skill and you will soon master it with a little practice. It makes your rolls nice and neat and it gives them added strength so they rise better. Once you have mastered moulding round, it will help you to make almost all the other shapes in this book.

If you can get into the habit of using two hands together when you work with portions of dough it will all go so much quicker. You should also notice those muscles on the outside of your upper arms protesting when you've got it right!

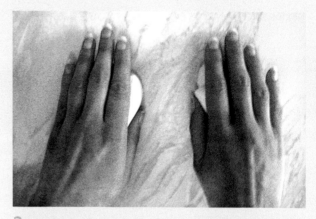

2 Put the whole of each palm on top of each portion of dough with your fingers out straight.

Step by step moulding round

1 Give each heap a quick knead on your work surface so you have a nice compact shape. You won't need to use extra flour – it would just make the dough slip.

3 With downward pressure from the whole of your palm – the whole time – begin to make small circular movements; the left hand will be going clockwise and the right hand anti-clockwise. As you continue making circles with downward pressure, cup your fingers around the dough.

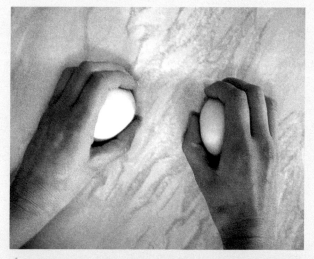

Solving problems

Some doughs are drier than others, which can make it difficult to mould them round as they tend to slip on the surface rather than spin. A mist of water on the work surface and on the top of the buns will solve this problem.

Very wet dough will require a little flour – but not too much or again it will just slip around on your work surface. Simply sprinkle some flour over the dough and the surface a little at a time.

Doughs with nuts or fruit in them have a tendency to lose their 'bits' as you mould them round. I just mould round and then mush the fruit into the bottom of the bun – fruit on top of buns always burns or becomes too chewy anyway.

Also, try not to be too heavy handed when moulding round dough that contains fruit or vegetables. Some of the pieces of fruit or vegetables will inevitably break up and smear into the dough, but if you treat it nice and gently you can minimise this.

4 Keep your fingers closely cupped around the dough (the little-finger side of your hands will rub on the work surface). Go round and round three or four more times until your dough is a nice smooth, round ball. When you pick up the dough and turn it over there will be a noticeable spiral on the bottom.

Rolling out rounds

For some shaped buns you will need to roll out the dough. Rest your dough, covered in clingfilm (plastic wrap), for 10 minutes before you start. Don't use brute force, just gentle rolls with even pressure and go round until you get the correct size. If the dough is resisting being rolled out, cover it and leave it for 5 minutes, then come back and try again.

Step by step rolling out rounds

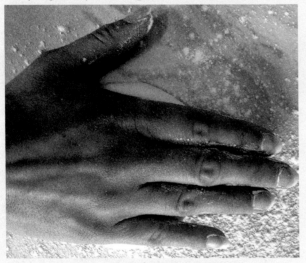

1 Place a portion of dough that has been moulded round and rested on a lightly floured work surface, then dust the top with flour. Flatten the ball of dough gently with the palm of your hand just to press the dough so it's a disc and not a ball.

2 Now you are going to start rolling, so keep these two things in mind: one, you will be rolling over the dough only once at each roll; two, as you roll over the dough and you come near the edge, decrease your downward pressure just a little so that when you roll off the edge of the dough you don't mash it down thinner than the rest of the dough.

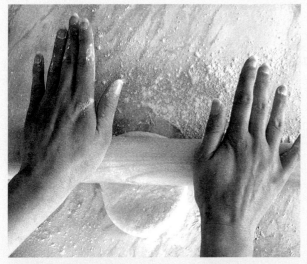

3 Using a rolling pin, start in the middle of the dough and, with even and fairly gentle downward pressure, push the rolling pin once over the dough away from you.

5 Pick up the dough, give it a quick dusting of flour and give the dough a quarter turn – whether clockwise or anti-clockwise is up to you, just stick to one direction.

4 Now go back to the middle and roll once over the bottom half of the dough – this time rolling towards you and easing off on the downward pressure before you roll off the end of the dough.

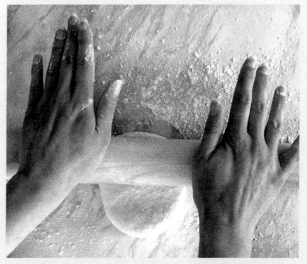

6 Repeat the rolling, then give another quarter turn and a dusting of flour if it needs it and carry on rolling and turning until you reach the diameter you need.

Rolling out sausages

For some recipes you will need to roll out sausages of dough. Use even pressure and continuous motion, not brute force or you will tear the dough and the sausage won't be an even thickness. If the dough is resisting being rolled out, cover it and leave it for 5 minutes, then come back and try again.

Step by step rolling out sausages

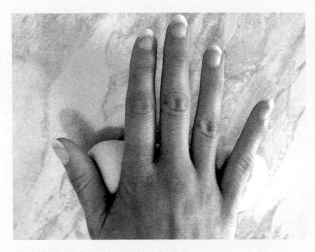

1 Place a portion of dough that has been moulded round and rested on a work surface (don't dust with any flour or it will just slip). Starting with one hand, push it from a round ball to a fat sausage.

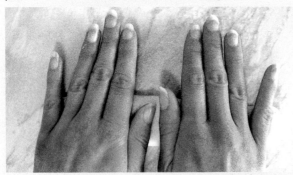

2 Place two hands on the sausage, press down gently and push the dough away from you and then gently roll it back towards you, still pressing down gently.

3 As you press down and push the dough away from you again, move your hands slightly apart from each other.

4 Continue this rolling and separating of your hands until your hands reach opposite ends of the dough. Straighten your arms to get the maximum amount out of each roll. Go back to the middle of the sausage and repeat the process until you reach the length and thickness you need.

Rolling out a rectangle

For some recipes you will need to roll out a rectangle. Don't be afraid to shift or lift up the dough and dust the work surface with flour, or even flip the dough over. Just lift carefully and avoid stretching the dough. If the dough resists being rolled out, cover it and leave it for 5 minutes, then come back and try again.

Step by step to rolling out a rectangle

1 Place a portion of dough that has been moulded round and rested on a lightly floured work surface, then dust the dough with flour. Push the ball of dough into fat sausage shape (see page 20).

3 With your rolling pin, start in the centre of the sausage and roll away from you with even downward pressure, easing off before you roll off the end. Repeat from the centre, this time rolling towards you.

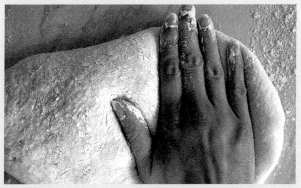

2 Gently flatten the sausage evenly with the palm of your hand.

4 Now give the dough a quarter turn. Place your rolling pin in the middle of the dough and roll away

from yourself as you did before. Go back to the middle and repeat, rolling towards you. Carry on rolling and turning the dough in this way, giving the dough and the work surface dustings of flour as they need it.

5 The corners have a tendency to become rounded so you need to move the dough from the centre to the outside to even out the length and thickness and square up the corners. Take hold of the middle of one of the wide edges of the dough with both hands with your thumbs on top and your fingers underneath. Gently clamp the dough between your fingers and palms, working your hands away from each other towards either end. Repeat this for the other wide side and then the narrow edges. You can do this at any time and as often as you need to.

6 Carry on rolling out the dough until you reach the correct size.

Chopping ingredients into the bread dough

The easiest way to distribute nuts, fruit, peel, vegetables and so on into your bread dough is to chop in the ingredients with your metal scraper (see page 10). This is an important technique as lots of my breads contain extra ingredients. There are several advantages to chopping the ingredients into your dough rather than kneading them in.

To begin with, you can see all the bits as you chop through and you can easily tell if they are evenly spread throughout the dough. Chopping in fruit or soft vegetables lessens the damage to the ingredients, helps to stop the smearing of strong colours and avoids creating too much moisture, which makes the dough hard to work with and ruins its finished texture. Whole nuts survive really well and, again, you can see whether or not they are evenly distributed.

Step by step to chopping in ingredients

3 Mound up your rough pieces, twisting and turning them about so the ingredients start to become evenly distributed. There is no need to press everything together into a solid lump.

1 Take the dough out of the mixing bowl and press it out into a rough round, about 2.5 cm/1 in thick, on top of your work surface. Pile the ingredients you wish to chop in on top of the dough, then fold the dough in on itself to encase the ingredients.

2 Using your metal scraper, chop right through the dough until it is chopped into rough pieces about 5 cm/2 in thick.

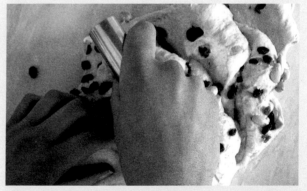

4 Now chop all the way through the mound of dough and ingredients again. Move all the pieces around again to help distribute the ingredients within the dough. Keep repeating this action until you feel the ingredients are evenly distributed throughout the dough. It usually takes about four or five goes to mix in the ingredients evenly.

Using a bread machine

I don't use a bread machine. With a mixer, I can have complete control over the process of making my loaves and can easily make adjustments as I go along to make sure everything is just right. But if you are used to using a breadmaker and prefer to let it do the work for you, then go right ahead!

Of course, you can only get the wonderful shapes and finishes of my original loaves if you finish them by hand, which means for some breads the machine would be used only for the mixing, kneading and first rising, then you finish them according to the recipes.

If you do want to use a breadmaker, you can adapt most of my recipes to make them in your machine. Here are some principles you will need to remember. Look at these in combination with your manufacturer's instructions and follow the guidelines in the recipes.

Which programme to use

Each machine has a slightly different range of programmes, so you will need to check the manufacturer's instructions in order to decide which is the most appropriate programme to use for specific recipes. However, you can make most recipes in the basic range of programmes you will find on the most straightforward machines.

Basic programme: Use this for most breads.

Wholemeal/wholewheat programme: This is best for breads made with wholemeal or heavier flours.

French/continental/speciality: Use this programme for French or Italian breads or breads with a very low fat content.

Dough: Use this for recipes when you are going to shape the dough and bake it in the oven. You will often need to allow the dough a second rising outside the machine once shaped. This is the most used option in this book, as I love to shape my loaves rather than having them all the same.

Other features

- On some machines, there is a colour crust option so you can choose how your finished loaf will look.
- Others may have an Extra Bake option so you can give the bread a bit longer to cook if it appears pale or not quite cooked when the programme has finished.

- Most machines have a buzzer that sounds after the first kneading to let you know it's time to add extra ingredients such as seeds or nuts. Some have a drawer for extra ingredients, tipping them in half way through the kneading process. Don't use this for wet ingredients as they will stick in the drawer.
- Some machines have a time-delay option so you can calculate when you want your bread to be ready for, say, breakfast.

Keep the yeast separate

It is essential to separate the yeast from the liquid ingredients when putting your ingredients into the dough pan. Some manufacturers suggest you put the liquid in first, some suggest you put the dry ingredients in first – the important thing is that the yeast does not get wet until the dough is mixed. I suggest you put the liquid ingredients in first, followed by the dry ingredients, then finally the yeast.

   For best results, use easy-blend yeast for loaves made on the Dough programme that you leave in the machine to mix and knead, then shape and bake in the oven. Use ordinary dried yeast for loaves made on the Basic programme, but there's no need to activate it first.

Other tips

- You can usually use cold liquid as it will be warmed by the machine before mixing. If you are using a Rapid or Fast programme, you do need to use warm liquid but make sure it is no hotter than tepid as the machine won't work if it is too hot.
- Always check the ingredients a couple of minutes after mixing starts and scrape down the sides with a plastic (never metal) spatula to prevent a build-up of flour around the edges, taking care not to touch the rotating blades.
- You may need to add a little more liquid to my doughs when using a breadmaker. You will need to experiment with your machine. Check after 5 minutes' kneading.
- Most breadmakers allow 1 hour for the first rising, so if I recommend more than that for a particular recipe, I have suggested that you leave the dough in the breadmaker for a further 30 minutes or 1 hour to continue to rise. The machine will still be warm enough for the dough to continue rising.
- Don't be tempted to open the lid during baking as you'll lose heat from the machine.
- The only time you should open the lid is to add nuts or other ingredients after the first kneading.

Baking your loaves

Most loaves are baked in a fairly hot oven so, for best results, always preheat the oven before you put your loaf in to bake. All ovens vary a bit, so use the temperatures given in the recipes as a starting point but be aware that you may need to make minor adjustments. You will know your own oven best.

Put the loaf in the oven, close the door and remember not to open it during the initial baking or the bread could collapse. Do keep an eye on the bread, though, towards the end of its cooking time – having a glass oven door is a great advantage here. Check a few minutes before the end of the cooking time: you may need to turn the sheet or tin (pan) to allow the bread to colour more evenly or you may need to take out the bread or leave it in a bit longer.

When bread is baked it sounds hollow when the base is tapped and feels a little lighter than when it went into the oven.

Notes on the recipes

Take a look at these notes before you start as they contain some useful principles that I apply when I am baking. Much of it is common sense and, with a little practice, you will soon get used to my ideas and my simple but accurate method.

- As I mentioned in the introductory text, it is much more accurate to weigh all but the very smallest quantities of ingredients. That is how you will get the best results. I've outlined my quick-and-easy method on page 12. Personally, I always measure in grams.
- For small quantities of ingredients, I do use measuring spoons. All spoon measurements are level.
- Do not mix metric and imperial. Follow one set only.
- American terms are given in brackets.
- The ingredients are listed in the order in which they are used in the recipe.
- Eggs are medium unless otherwise stated. If you use a different size, adjust the amount of liquid or flour added to obtain the right consistency.
- See full kneading and shaping instructions on pages 14–22.
- You will always need a little extra flour for dusting and sometimes a little extra water to obtain the right consistency.
- Always wash, peel, core and seed, if necessary, fresh foods before use. Ensure that all produce is as fresh as possible and in good condition.
- All ovens vary, so cooking times have to be approximate. Adjust cooking times and temperatures according to your manufacturer's instructions and check your loaves just before the completion of the cooking time.
- Always preheat a conventional oven and cook on the centre shelf unless otherwise specified. Although fan ovens do not usually require preheating, I prefer to give it a good 10 minutes – that first 'spring' of the dough in the oven is very important.

PERFECT LOAVES

'Oooh, that looks good!'
That's the first thing I say when
I see a freshly baked loaf of
bread. Then, of course, I have to
get nearer to inhale all that
incredible aroma.

I really am mad about bread;
it's just so exciting, and it never
ceases to amaze me how many
different ways it can be formed
and how many different
flavours can be incorporated.
But, even though you can let
your imagination run wild and
produce fantastic results, I think
everyone also loves a simple,
perfect loaf fresh from the oven.
So this is a chapter of simple,
wholesome loaves that are perfect
for sandwiches and toast.

Beautiful White Plait

This is an enriched loaf with a soft crust and wonderful, full flavour. It looks beautiful – you'll see what I mean when you take it out of the oven! It also makes fantastic toast. If you want to slice a loaf it is best to let it cool almost completely first – but if you are going to eat hunks with cheese and butter just let it cool a bit.

MAKES 1 LARGE LOAF

650 g/1 lb 7 oz strong white bread flour
35 g/1¼ oz caster (superfine) sugar
15 g/½ oz salt

15 g/½ oz dried milk powder (non-fat dry milk)
1 sachet of easy-blend dried yeast
1 egg, beaten

50 g/1¾ oz butter, melted
300 g/10½ oz warm water

1. Place all the ingredients in your mixer bowl and combine with the dough hook on speed 1 for 2 minutes or until you have soft dough that doesn't smear the bottom of the bowl. If necessary, add a little more flour or water, no more than 15 g/½ oz at a time, until you reach the desired consistency.

2. Mix on speed 2 for 10 minutes. Keep an eye on the consistency throughout; it is better if the dough is a bit too soft than adding too much flour.

3. Take the dough out of the mixer, knead it a few times and shape it into a head (see page 14).

4. Place the dough back into the mixing bowl, cover with clingfilm (plastic wrap) and a tea towel (dish cloth) and leave to rise for 1 hour. The dough won't rise very much.

5. Knock the dough back, knead it a few times and reshape it into a head. Re-cover the dough and leave to rise for another hour. The dough will have only risen a little (I know it seems ages but it's worth it to develop the bread's flavour and texture).

6   Grease and flour a 33 x 30 cm/13 x 12 in baking (cookie) sheet or just line with non-stick liner.

7   Divide the dough into three equal portions. Mould the three portions round (see pages 16–17), cover and leave to relax for 10 minutes. If you find the portions of dough are too big for your hands using the moulding round technique, then use the moulding into a head method (see page 14).

8   Roll out each portion into a 56 cm/22 in sausage (see page 20); you shouldn't need any extra flour as the dough isn't sticky. Repeat with the other two portions, keeping the portions not in use covered.

9   Now you are going to plait the sausages. Place all three sausages side by side in front of you. Place the three ends one on top of each other and pinch them together very firmly. In case you don't know how to plait, it's very easy to do. Number the sausages one, two, three from the left; you are going to move the sausages but the number positions stay the same, so two is always in the middle. Take sausage number three and place it over sausage number two. Then take sausage number one and place it over sausage number two, then just repeat three over two then one over two and keep going. When you are plaiting try not to pull the sausages, just place them together closely. Don't be afraid to shift, lift or readjust either the sausages or the plait to make it look good and to make it easier for you to work with.

10 When the ends of the sausages become short and you cannot comfortably take one sausage over another, gather them all one on top of the other – as you did to start – and pinch them very firmly together. Now tuck both the pinched ends about 2.5 cm/1 in under the loaf until they look neat. Give the whole loaf a couple of gentle rolls – just push it forward and bring it back two or three times – to help settle the loaf. It should be about 40 cm/16 in long.

11 Lift the loaf and, without stretching it, place it diagonally on the prepared baking sheet, making sure the ends are still tucked in and the loaf is in a nice straight line. Again, you can shift, lift and move the loaf about. Sprinkle the loaf with a little bread flour (to prevent the clingfilm sticking) and then cover with clingfilm and a tea towel. Allow to rise for 1½ hours.

12 About 15 minutes before the end of the rising time, preheat the oven to 200°C/400°F/gas 6/fan oven 180°C.

13 Uncover the loaf and evenly, but without being heavy handed, sprinkle the loaf again with bread flour. You can sift it over or just sprinkle the flour from your fingers, from about 25 cm/10 in above the loaf.

14 Bake for 10 minutes. Then, without opening the oven door, turn the heat down to 180°C/350°F/gas 4/fan oven 160°C and bake for a further 15 minutes until the loaf is golden and the bottom sounds hollow when you tap it.

15 Transfer to a wire rack to cool. Beautiful, isn't it!

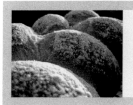

BREADMAKER TIPS
To make the dough, put the liquid ingredients in first, then the dry ingredients, adding the yeast last. Use the Dough programme to mix the dough and allow it to rise. Leave it in the breadmaker for an extra 30 minutes to continue to rise, then remove from the breadmaker and continue from step 6.

Butter-scented Soft White Round

This is perfect for sandwiches and toast and brushing with butter provides a beautiful golden colour, a soft crust and a lovely smell. As the loaf cools, the top crust will crinkle a bit. In a breadmaker, you can use the Basic programme, omitting the butter; or the Dough programme, leaving it to rise for an extra 30 minutes then continuing from step 5.

MAKES 1 LARGE LOAF

500 g/1 lb 2 oz strong white bread flour

10 g/2 tsp salt
5 g/1 tsp caster (superfine) sugar
1 sachet of easy-blend dried yeast

15 g/½ oz butter, melted
300 g/10½ oz warm water
20 g/¾ oz melted butter, for brushing

1   Place all the ingredients except the melted butter for brushing in your mixer bowl and combine with the dough hook on speed 1 for 2 minutes or until you have soft dough that doesn't smear the bottom of the bowl. If necessary, add a little more flour or water, no more than 15 g/½ oz at a time, until you reach the desired consistency.

2   Mix on speed 2 for 10 minutes and check frequently during this time to maintain a soft dough that isn't smearing on the bottom.

3   Mould the dough into a head (see page 14) and place it back in the mixing bowl. Cover the bowl with clingfilm (plastic wrap) and a tea towel (dish cloth). This dough has a slightly sticky texture so use a little flour only if you need to.

4   Let the dough rise for about 1½ hours or until doubled in size. (In the winter you may need to leave it to rise for 2 hours.)

5   Take the dough out of the mixing bowl, knead it a bit (you may need a light dusting of flour), shape it into a head, cover and let it rest for 5 minutes.

6   Grease and flour a 33 x 30 cm/13 x 12 in baking (cookie) sheet or just line with non-stick liner.

7   With a little flour for dusting, roll the dough to a 18 cm/7 in round (see pages 18–19). Place the round on the prepared baking sheet and dust the top very lightly with a little flour. Cover the dough with clingfilm and a tea towel. Allow the dough to rise for 45 minutes.

8   About 15 minutes before the end of the rising time, preheat the oven to 200°C/400°F/gas 6/fan oven 180°C.

9   Very gently remove the tea towel and clingfilm from the round. Brush the top and sides of the round with the melted butter.

10   Bake for 25–27 minutes until the loaf is lightly golden and the bottom sounds hollow when you tap it.

11   Transfer to a wire rack to cool.

Butter-scented Soft Brown Round

I really like egg and cress sandwiches and, in my opinion, this soft wholemeal loaf suits the combination perfectly, especially as it cuts so well. In a breadmaker, you can use the Basic programme, omitting the butter; or the Dough programme, leaving it to rise for an extra 30 minutes then continuing from step 5.

MAKES 1 LARGE LOAF

500 g/1 lb 2 oz wholemeal bread flour

15 g/¹⁄₂ oz salt

5 g/1 tsp caster (superfine) sugar

1 sachet of easy-blend dried yeast

15 g/¹⁄₂ oz butter, melted

310 g/11 oz warm water

20 g/³⁄₄ oz melted butter, for brushing

1 Place all the ingredients except the melted butter for brushing in your mixer bowl and combine with the dough hook on speed 1 for 2 minutes or until you have soft dough that doesn't smear the bottom of the bowl. If necessary, add a little more flour or water, no more than 15 g/¹⁄₂ oz at a time, until you reach the desired consistency.

2 Mix on speed 2 for 10 minutes and check frequently during this time to maintain a soft dough that isn't smearing on the bottom.

3 Mould the dough into a head (see page 14) and place it back in the mixing bowl. Cover the bowl with clingfilm (plastic wrap) and a tea towel (dish cloth). This dough has a slightly sticky texture, so use a little flour only if you need to.

4 Let the dough rise for about 1¹⁄₂ hours or until doubled in size. (In the winter you may need to leave it to rise for 2 hours.)

5 Take the dough out of the mixing bowl, knead it a bit (you may need a light dusting of flour), shape it into a head, cover and let it rest for 5 minutes.

6 Grease and flour a 33 x 30 cm/13 x 12 in baking (cookie) sheet or just line with non-stick liner.

7 With a little flour for dusting, roll the dough to a 18 cm/7 in round (see pages 16–17). Place the round on the prepared baking sheet and dust the top very lightly with a little flour. Cover the dough with clingfilm and a tea towel. Allow the dough to rise for 45 minutes.

8 About 15 minutes before the end of the rising time, preheat the oven to 200°C/400°F/gas 6/fan oven 180°C.

9 Very gently remove the tea towel and clingfilm from the round. Brush the top and sides of the round with the melted butter.

10 Bake for 25–27 minutes until the loaf is lightly golden and the bottom sounds hollow when you tap it.

11 Transfer to a wire rack to cool.

Butter-scented Soft Granary Round

The sound of the grains in the granary flour hitting the mixing bowl when they are weighed in is a hint of how good the finished loaf will be! Give it a try – I'm sure you won't be disappointed. In a breadmaker, you can use the Basic or Wholemeal programme, omitting the butter; or the Dough programme, leaving it to rise for an extra 30 minutes then continuing from step 5.

MAKES 1 LARGE LOAF

500 g/1 lb 2 oz granary bread flour

10 g/2 tsp salt
5 g/1 tsp caster (superfine) sugar
1 sachet of easy-blend dried yeast

15 g/½ oz butter, melted
300 g/10½ oz warm water
20 g/¾ oz melted butter, for brushing

1 Place all the ingredients except the melted butter for brushing in your mixer bowl and combine with the dough hook on speed 1 for 2 minutes or until you have soft dough that doesn't smear the bottom of the bowl. If necessary, add a little more flour or water, no more than 15 g/½ oz at a time, until you reach the desired consistency.

2 Mix on speed 2 for 10 minutes and check frequently during this time to maintain a soft dough that isn't smearing on the bottom.

3 Mould the dough into a head (see page 14) and place it back in the mixing bowl. Cover the bowl with clingfilm (plastic wrap) and a tea towel (dish cloth). This dough has a slightly sticky texture, so use a little flour only if you need to.

4 Let the dough rise for about 1½ hours or until doubled in size. (In the winter you may need to leave it to rise for 2 hours.)

5 Take the dough out of the mixing bowl, knead it a bit (you may need a light dusting of flour), shape it into a head, cover and let it rest for 5 minutes.

6 Grease and flour a 33 x 30 cm/13 x 12 in baking (cookie) sheet or just line with non-stick liner.

7 With a little flour for dusting, roll the dough to a 18 cm/7 in round (see pages 16–17). Place the round on the prepared baking sheet and dust the top very lightly with a little flour. Cover the dough with clingfilm and a tea towel. Allow the dough to rise for 45 minutes.

8 About 15 minutes before the end of the rising time, preheat the oven to 200°C/400°F/gas 6/fan oven 180°C.

9 Very gently remove the tea towel and clingfilm from the round. Brush the top and sides of the round with the melted butter.

10 Bake for 25–28 minutes until the loaf is lightly golden and the bottom sounds hollow when you tap it.

11 Transfer to a wire rack to cool.

Wholemeal and Oatmeal Loaf

This is a really good sandwich loaf. I especially like to use it for chicken sandwiches – one of my favourites – as the flavours of the poultry and the bread complement each other well. In a breadmaker, you can use the Basic or Wholemeal programme, sprinkling on the oats after the rising; or the Dough programme, leaving it to rise for an extra 1 hour then continuing from step 5.

MAKES 1 LOAF

FOR THE DOUGH
360 g/12¾ oz wholemeal bread flour
35 g/1¼ oz porridge oats

7.5 g/1½ tsp salt
35 g/1¼ oz dark muscovado sugar
5 g/1 tsp dried milk powder (non-fat dry milk)
1 sachet of easy-blend dried yeast

15 g/½ oz butter, melted
1 egg, beaten
185 g/6½ oz warm water
FOR THE TOPPING
40 g/1½ oz jumbo oats

1   Place all the dough ingredients in your mixer bowl and combine with the dough hook on speed 1 for 2 minutes or until you have soft dough that doesn't smear the bottom of the bowl. If necessary, add a little more flour or water, no more than 15 g/½ oz at a time, until you reach the desired consistency.

2   Mix on speed 2 for 10 minutes. Keep an eye on the consistency and add a little flour or water if needed.

3   Mould the dough into a head (see page 14) and place it back in the mixing bowl, cover with clingfilm (plastic wrap) and a tea towel (dish cloth).

4   Let the dough rise for 2 hours or until doubled in size.

5   Grease and flour a 33 x 30 cm/13 x 12 in baking (cookie) sheet or just line with non-stick liner. Place the jumbo oats on a large plate.

6   Take the risen dough out of the bowl and mould it back into a head.

7   With a rolling pin, working in quarter turns, gently roll the dough into an 18 cm/7 in round (see pages 18–19). Use a little flour if you need to.

8   Brush the top of the loaf with water. Place the loaf, wet side down, on the plate of jumbo oats. Gently press the loaf down, carefully pick the loaf up and turn it right side up, letting the loose jumbo oats fall back on to the plate. Place the loaf on the prepared baking sheet.

9   Cover the loaf with clingfilm and a tea towel and allow to rise for 1½ hours.

10 About 15 minutes before the end of the rising time, preheat the oven to 200°C/400°F/gas 6/fan oven 180°C.

11 Bake the loaf for 25–28 minutes until it sounds hollow when you tap the base.

12 Transfer to a wire rack to cool.

Tropical Wholemeal and Rye Loaf

This loaf is slightly sweet and packed full of flavour, the rye flour giving it a slightly denser texture than an ordinary wholemeal loaf, while the dates and nuts make it wonderfully delicious and moist. I think this bread tastes great just as it is, or you can spread it with a little butter if you prefer.

MAKES 1 LARGE LOAF

FOR THE DOUGH
360 g/12¾ oz wholemeal bread flour
100 g/3½ oz rye flour
5 g/1 tsp salt
70 g/2½ oz dark muscovado sugar

5 g/1 tsp dried milk powder (non-fat dry milk)
1 sachet of easy-blend dried yeast
10 g/2 tsp vanilla essence (extract)
15 g/½ oz butter, melted
1 egg, beaten
200 g/7 oz warm water

FOR THE FILLING
100 g/3½ oz brazil nuts
100 g/3½ oz sugar-rolled or ready-to-eat dates, roughly chopped
FOR THE TOPPING
15 g/½ oz butter, melted
20 g/¾ oz vanilla sugar

1 Place all the dough ingredients in your mixer bowl and combine with the dough hook on speed 1 for 2 minutes or until you have soft dough that doesn't smear the bottom of the bowl. If necessary, add a little more flour or water, no more than 15 g/½ oz at a time, until you reach the desired consistency.

2 Mix on speed 2 for 7 minutes, adding wholemeal bread flour as needed to maintain the correct dough consistency. Try to add as little as possible.

3 Mould the dough into a head (see page 14), place it back in the mixing bowl and cover with clingfilm (plastic wrap) and a tea towel (dish cloth). Leave to rise for 2 hours or until doubled in size. The dough will seem a bit sticky and heavy but that's fine.

4 Meanwhile, grease and flour a 33 x 30 cm/13 x 12 in baking (cookie) sheet or just line with non-stick liner. Toast the brazil nuts in a preheated oven at 180°C/350°F/gas 4/fan oven 160°C for 7–8 minutes. Allow them to cool, then chop them roughly and mix with the chopped dates. Turn off the oven.

5   Take the dough out of the bowl, flatten it out a bit on your work surface and pile the nuts and dates on top of it. Wrap the dough over the filling to encase it and use your metal scraper to chop the filling into the dough (see page 23). Mould the dough back into a head, cover and allow to rest for 5 minutes.

6   Gently roll out the dough into a fat 28 cm/11 in sausage (see page 20), gently tapering the ends to make a torpedo shape. You shouldn't need any flour for dusting but, if you do, use a little rye flour.

7   Place the loaf on the prepared baking sheet and cover with clingfilm and a tea towel. Allow the bread to rise for 1½ hours.

8   About 15 minutes before the end of the rising time, preheat the oven to 200°C/400°F/gas 6/fan oven 180°C.

9   Bake the loaf for 40–45 minutes until it sounds hollow when you tap the base.

10   Transfer to a wire rack. While it is still hot from the oven, brush the loaf all over with melted butter, then sprinkle the vanilla sugar over the entire loaf.

BREADMAKER TIPS

To make the dough, put the liquid ingredients in first with an extra 15 g/1 tbsp of liquid, then the dry ingredients, adding the yeast last. Either bake the loaf using the Basic or Wholemeal programme, adding the filling ingredients after the first rising, or use the Dough programme to mix the dough and allow it to rise. Leave it in the breadmaker for an extra 1 hour to continue to rise, then remove from the breadmaker and continue from step 4.

Wholemeal, Seeds and Rye Loaf

The texture of this delicious and nutritious bread is closer than white bread or even wholemeal but it really is delicious. The toasted sunflower and pumpkin seeds give it lots of flavour and texture. The dough will feel a bit heavy and sticky as you work with it, but don't worry – it will all turn out right in the end!

MAKES 1 LARGE LOAF

FOR THE DOUGH
360 g/12¼ oz wholemeal bread flour
100 g/3½ oz rye flour
5 g/1 tsp salt
50 g/1¾ oz dark muscovado sugar

5 g/1 tsp dried milk powder (non-fat dry milk)
7.5 g/1½ tsp caraway seeds
1 sachet of easy-blend dried yeast
15 g/½ oz butter, melted
1 egg, beaten
300 g/8 oz warm water

FOR THE FILLING
50 g/1¾ oz sunflower seeds
50 g/1¾ oz pumpkin seeds
FOR THE TOPPING
Rye flour, for dusting

1. Place all the dough ingredients in your mixer bowl and combine with the dough hook on speed 1 for 2 minutes or until you have soft dough that doesn't smear the bottom of the bowl.

2. Add 15 g/½ oz of warm water and mix on speed 2 for 7 minutes. The dough should become very soft, and that's how it should be so don't add any more flour.

3. Mould the dough into a head (see page 14) and place it back in the mixing bowl, cover with clingfilm (plastic wrap) and a tea towel (dish cloth).

4. Let the dough rise for 2 hours.

5. Meanwhile, grease and flour a 33 x 30 cm/ 13 x 12 in baking (cookie) sheet or just line with non-stick liner. Toast the sunflower and pumpkin seeds in a preheated oven at 180°C/350°F/gas 4/ fan oven 160°C for 6–7 minutes. Remove from the oven and allow to cool. Turn off the oven.

6. Take the dough out of the bowl, flatten it out a bit on your work surface and pile the seeds on top of it. Wrap the dough over the seeds to

encase them and use your metal scraper to chop all the way through the dough until the seeds look evenly distributed (see page 23).

7   Knead the dough until it comes together, then mould it back into a head.

8   With a rolling pin, working in quarter turns, gently roll the dough into a 15 cm/6 in round (see pages 18–19), using a little rye flour if you need to.

9   Place the loaf on the prepared baking sheet and cover with clingfilm and a tea towel. Allow the bread to rise for 1½ hours.

10 About 15 minutes before the end of the rising time, preheat the oven to 200°C/400°F/gas 6/fan oven 180°C.

11 Sprinkle the top of the loaf evenly with rye flour, without being heavy handed. Bake the loaf for 40–45 minutes until it sounds hollow when you tap the base.

12 Transfer to a wire rack and allow to cool for at least 30 minutes before slicing.

BREADMAKER TIPS

To make the dough, put the liquid ingredients in first, then the dry ingredients, adding the yeast last. Either bake the loaf using the Basic or Wholemeal programme with a medium crust, adding the filling ingredients after the first rising, or use the Dough programme to mix the dough and allow it to rise. Leave it in the breadmaker for an extra 1 hour to continue to rise, then remove from the breadmaker and continue from step 5.

Halloween Pumpkin Bread – Seeds and All!

The idea of carving a pumpkin-shaped bread with seeds and all – especially at Halloween – appealed to my sense of humour! Do allow time to make the pumpkin purée – I usually make it the day before – but you can use ready-made. It freezes very well but, before using it, you should pour away any excess liquid that comes out as it defrosts.

MAKES 1 LOAF

FOR THE PUMPKIN PURÉE
300 g/11 oz wedge of pumpkin (squash)
FOR THE DOUGH
425 g/15 oz strong white bread flour
10 g/2 tsp dried milk powder (non-fat dry milk)
½ tsp salt
50 g/1¾ oz light muscovado sugar

7.5 g/1½ tsp ground cinnamon
¼ tsp grated nutmeg
½ tsp ground ginger
⅛ tsp ground cloves
1 sachet of easy-blend dried yeast
½ tsp vanilla essence (extract)
1 egg, beaten
30 g/1 oz butter, melted
100 g/3½ oz warm water

FOR THE FILLING
40 g/1½ oz pumpkin seeds
½ tsp ground cinnamon
25 g/1 oz light muscovado sugar
15 g/½ oz butter
¼ tsp vanilla essence (extract)
FOR THE EGG WASH
1 egg yolk mixed with 15 g/½ oz water
Icing (confectioners') sugar, for dusting

1 Cut the pumpkin flesh into 5 cm/2 in chunks and steam for 35–40 minutes until tender. Purée in a food processor, then transfer to a sieve (strainer) set over a bowl and allow the excess moisture to drain away. This will take about 2 hours. Make sure the purée is at room temperature before adding it to the rest of the ingredients when you start making the dough.

2 Place 100 g/3½ oz of the prepared pumpkin purée and all the dough ingredients in your mixer bowl and combine with the dough hook on speed 1 for 2 minutes or until you have soft dough that doesn't smear the bottom of the bowl.

3 Mix on speed 2 for 10 minutes, maintaining a soft dough but, if it starts to smear the bottom of the bowl, add a little bread flour, no more than 15 g/½ oz at a time, until you reach the desired consistency.

4 Take the dough out of the mixer, knead it a few times (it will have a sticky texture) and mould it

into a head (see page 14). Place it back in the mixing bowl, cover with clingfilm (plastic wrap) and a tea towel (dish cloth) and leave to rise for 1½ hours.

5 Meanwhile, grease and flour a 33 x 30 cm/13 x 12 in baking (cookie) sheet or just line with non-stick liner. Lightly toast the pumpkin seeds on an ungreased baking sheet in a preheated oven at 180°C/350°F/gas 4/fan oven 160°C for 5 minutes. Remove the seeds from the oven and turn off the oven.

6 Divide the dough into two portions, one 420 g/ 14½ oz and the other 340 g/11½ oz, sharing around any extra dough. Mould the larger portion round (see pages 16–17).

7 To make the filling, combine the toasted pumpkin seeds, cinnamon and sugar and set to one side. Melt the butter and add the vanilla, then set to one side.

8 Using a rolling pin, roll out the larger portion of dough to an 28 cm/11 in round (see pages 18–19). Place the round on your prepared baking sheet.

9 Using your metal scraper, chop the pumpkin seed mixture into the smaller portion of dough (see page 23), then chop in the butter and vanilla. Chop the pieces fairly small.

10 Place the filled dough in a neat pile in the centre of your 28 cm/11 in round. Dampen the edge of the round with water.

11 Gather up the round and bring it together over the filling into a scrunched top. Allow the dough to pleat over itself as you bring up the edges. Pinch the top together firmly but leave some slack between the stem and the filling – the bread will rise and fill up the slack (if you scrunch the top too tightly next to the filling, it will tear itself open in the oven). Pinch the top to tidy it and make it look more like a stem.

12 Cover the bread and allow it to rise for 20 minutes while you preheat the oven to 200°C/400°F/gas 6/fan oven 180°C.

13 Brush the entire loaf with egg wash, then bake for 35–40 minutes until a deep golden colour.

14 Transfer to a wire rack and allow the loaf to cool a bit. Don't worry if the dough has torn open a bit in the oven – some icing sugar will hide it!

15 Carve out eyes and a mouth with a sharp knife if you wish and dust the top with icing sugar. Carve the pumpkin at the table and serve in wedges.

BREADMAKER TIPS

To make the dough, put the liquid ingredients in first, then the dry ingredients, adding the yeast last. Use the Dough programme to mix the dough and allow it to rise. Leave it in the breadmaker for an extra 30 minutes to continue to rise, then remove from the breadmaker and continue from step 5.

Olive Oil Wells

This is so easy to make and absolutely delicious, with the wonderful Mediterranean flavour of a good-quality olive oil. I'm always tempted to eat one slice too many – even though it is very filling! In a breadmaker, you can use the Dough programme, leaving it to rise for an extra 1 hour then continuing from step 5.

MAKES 1 LARGE LOAF

FOR THE DOUGH
500 g/1 lb 2 oz strong white bread flour
10 g/2 tsp salt
20 g/³/₄ oz caster (superfine) sugar
5 g/1 tsp dried milk powder (non-fat dry milk)
1 sachet of easy-blend dried yeast
50 g/1³/₄ oz extra virgin olive oil
250 g/9 oz warm water

FOR THE TOPPING
40 g/1½ oz extra virgin olive oil

1 Place all the dough ingredients in your mixer bowl and combine with the dough hook on speed 1 for 2 minutes or until you have soft dough that doesn't smear the bottom of the bowl. If necessary, add a little more flour or water, no more than 15 g/½ oz at a time, until you reach the desired consistency.

2 Mix on speed 2 for 10 minutes; add a scant 15 g/½ oz of bread flour or water, as needed, to maintain the correct dough consistency.

3 Take the dough out of the mixer and knead it a bit. Mould it into a head (see page 14), place it back in the mixing bowl and cover with clingfilm (plastic wrap) and a tea towel (dish cloth).

4 Let the dough rise for 2 hours until doubled in size.

5 Knock back the dough, take it out of the mixing bowl, knead it a bit, then mould it back into a head. Re-cover and allow to rest for 10 minutes.

6 Meanwhile, grease and flour a 33 x 30 cm/ 13 x 12 in baking (cookie) sheet or just line with non-stick liner.

7 Using a rolling pin, roll out the dough to a 30 x 25 cm/12 x 10 in rectangle (see pages 21–2, but the edges can stay rounded if you like). Use white bread flour for dusting. Place the rectangle on the prepared baking sheet, cover with clingfilm and a tea towel and allow to rise for 30 minutes.

8 About 15 minutes before the end of the rising time, preheat the oven to 220°C/425°F/gas 7/fan oven 200°C.

9 Using your index finger, poke straight lines of holes into the risen dough, pressing down right to the baking sheet. The holes and the lines should be about 2.5 cm/1 in apart from each other. Drizzle the entire loaf with extra virgin olive oil, filling up all the wells.

10 Bake for 13–15 minutes until golden.

11 Transfer to a wire rack to cool.

Corn Rows

This is a really neat bread! It is light, but with a very interesting density, and just a little bit sweet. It's great served with anything with a bit of spiciness or bite, as it gives an excellent contrast of flavours. In a breadmaker, you can use the Dough programme, leaving it to rise for an extra 1 hour then continuing from step 5.

MAKES 1 LARGE LOAF

415 g/14½ oz strong white bread flour
100 g/3½ oz cornmeal, plus extra for sprinkling

10 g/2 tsp salt
40 g/1½ oz caster (superfine) sugar
10 g/2 tsp dried milk powder (non-fat dry milk)
1 sachet of easy-blend dried yeast

50 g/1¾ oz butter, melted
265 g/9½ oz warm water

1   Place all the ingredients in your mixer bowl and combine with the dough hook on speed 1 for 2 minutes or until you have soft dough that doesn't smear the bottom of the bowl. If necessary, add a little more flour or water, no more than 15 g/½ oz at a time, until you reach the desired consistency.

2   Mix on speed 2 for 10 minutes; add a scant 15 g/½ oz of bread flour, as needed, to maintain the correct dough consistency. The cornmeal will absorb a lot of water, so it is better to leave the dough a little soft than add too much flour.

3   Take the dough out of the mixer and knead it a bit. Mould it into a head (see page 14), place it back in the mixing bowl and cover with clingfilm (plastic wrap) and a tea towel (dish cloth).

4   Let the dough rise for 2 hours until doubled in size.

5   Knock the dough back, take it out of the mixing bowl, knead it a bit, then mould it back into a head. Re-cover and allow to rest for 10 minutes.

6   Meanwhile, grease and flour a 33 x 30 cm/13 x 12 in baking (cookie) sheet or just line with non-stick liner. Sprinkle the sheet evenly, but without being heavy handed, with cornmeal.

7   Using a rolling pin, roll out the dough to a 30 x 25 cm/12 x 10 in rectangle (see pages 21–2, but the edges of the rectangle can stay rounded). Use white bread flour for dusting. Place the rectangle on the baking sheet, cover with clingfilm and a tea towel and allow to rise for 30 minutes.

8   About 15 minutes before the end of rising, preheat the oven to 220°C/425°F/gas 7/fan oven 200°C.

9   Using the side of a clean ruler, mark 2.5 cm/1 in intervals along the length of the bread. Press the ruler through the dough almost to the baking sheet, but without cutting through it.

10 Bake for 15–20 minutes until lightly golden.

11 Transfer to a wire rack to cool.

Sesame Squares

I like to use these instead of hamburger buns as they go so well with burgers and grilled meats. Some seeds will slip off when you eat the bread, so use a large plate! In a breadmaker, you can use the Dough programme, leaving it to rise for an extra 1 hour then continuing from step 5. (See the photograph on page 25.)

MAKES 12 SQUARES

FOR THE DOUGH
500 g/1 lb 2 oz strong white bread flour
10 g/2 tsp salt
40 g/1½ oz caster (superfine) sugar

10 g/2 tsp dried milk powder (non-fat dry milk)
1 sachet of easy-blend dried yeast
50 g/1¾ oz toasted sesame oil
250 g/9 oz warm water
Cornmeal, for sprinkling

FOR THE TOPPING
20 g/¾ oz sesame seeds
½ tsp black onion seeds
15 g/½ oz toasted sesame oil, for brushing

1. Place all the dough ingredients in your mixer bowl and combine with the dough hook on speed 1 for 2 minutes or until you have soft dough that doesn't smear the bottom of the bowl. If necessary, add a little more flour or water, no more than 15 g/½ oz at a time, until you reach the desired consistency.

2. Mix on speed 2 for 10 minutes; add a scant 15 g/½ oz of bread flour, as needed, to maintain the correct dough consistency.

3. Take the dough out of the mixer and knead it a bit. Mould it into a head (see page 14), place it back in the mixing bowl and cover with clingfilm (plastic wrap) and a tea towel (dish cloth).

4. Let the dough rise for 2 hours (it won't rise a great deal).

5. Knock back the dough, take it out of the mixing bowl, knead it a bit, then mould it back into a head. Re-cover and allow to rest for 10 minutes.

6. Meanwhile, grease and flour a 33 x 30 cm/13 x 12 in baking (cookie) sheet or just line with non-stick liner. Sprinkle the sheet evenly, but without being heavy handed, with cornmeal.

7. Using a rolling pin, roll out the dough to a 30 x 25 cm/12 x 10 in rectangle (see pages 21–2, but the edges of the rectangle can stay rounded if you like). Use white bread flour for dusting. Place the rectangle on the prepared baking sheet, cover with clingfilm and a tea towel and allow to rise for 30 minutes.

8. About 15 minutes before the end of the rising time, preheat the oven to 220°C/425°F/gas 7/fan oven 200°C. Mix together the seeds.

9. Brush the top and sides of the loaf very gently with the sesame oil, then sprinkle the loaf evenly with the mixed seeds.

10. Using the side of a clean ruler, mark two lines at roughly 7.5 cm/3 in intervals along the longer side of the dough. Press the side of the ruler all the way through the dough almost to the baking sheet, but without cutting through it. Then make three lines at roughly 7.5 cm/3 in intervals along the shorter side of the bread. You will now have twelve (roughly) 7.5 cm/3 in squares.

11. Bake for 12–15 minutes until golden. Transfer to a wire rack to cool.

SANDWICH LOAVES

This bread makes wonderful little pull-apart sandwiches. Soft and buttery in the middle with a wonky, crunchy top.

When you take one of these loaves out of the oven, carefully tip it out of its tin (pan) on to a wire cooling rack. Gently ease the middle two sandwiches apart. The texture should be soft not uncooked. If it's not fully baked, give the loaf another 5 minutes, then test again.

Do come up with your own filling ideas – making sure they are pre-cooked and cooled if need be. But don't put too much filling in each sandwich; the bread is going to swell as it rises and if you have over filled it, it will just squeeze up out of the loaf in the oven.

After the bread has cooled for about 5 minutes, separate the loaves into sandwiches.

Bacon and Marmalade Sandwich Loaf

The sweet marmalade and the salty bacon work so well in this sandwich loaf. Use the best-quality marmalade you can – home-made if possible. In fact, it was while I was sampling the contents of a pot of my friend Gill's 'Old Farm Marm' that I first started thinking about this combination.

MAKES 2 LOAVES

FOR THE DOUGH
250 g/9 oz strong white bread flour
250 g/9 oz wholemeal bread flour
10 g/2 tsp caster (superfine) sugar
10 g/2 tsp dried milk powder (non-fat dry milk)

10 g/2 tsp salt
1 sachet + 1 tsp easy-blend dried yeast
10 g/2 tsp butter, melted
320 g/11¼ oz warm water

FOR THE FILLING
20 g/¾ oz butter
80 g/2¾ oz onion, very finely chopped (red is nice)

300 g/10½ oz smoked back bacon, chopped into approximately 2.5 cm/1 in pieces
140 g/5 oz marmalade
Freshly ground black pepper
30 g/1 oz butter, for brushing

1   Place all the dough ingredients in your mixer bowl and combine with the dough hook on speed 1 for 2 minutes or until you have soft dough that doesn't smear the bottom of the bowl. If necessary, add a little more flour or water, no more than 15 g/½ oz at a time, until you reach the desired consistency.

2   Mix on speed 2 for 10 minutes. Keep an eye on the consistency throughout; better a bit too soft than adding too much flour.

3   Take the dough out of the mixer, knead it a few times and mould it into a head (see page 14). Place the dough back in the mixing bowl, cover with clingfilm (plastic wrap) and a tea towel (dish cloth) and leave to rise for 1 hour.

4   Meanwhile, grease and flour two 450 g/1 lb 20 x 10 cm/8 x 4 in loaf tins (pans).

5   To prepare the filling, melt the butter in a small frying pan (skillet) over a medium heat. Add the onion to the pan and cook for about 4 minutes. Then add the bacon and cook for about 2–4 minutes, stirring frequently, until the bacon is

cooked and the onions are tender. Add the marmalade and stir just until it has melted. Take the pan off the heat and season with pepper to taste. Set aside to cool.

6 Divide the dough into eight 105 g/3½ oz portions and share around any leftover dough equally between the portions. Mould round (see pages 16–17), cover and allow to rest for 5 minutes. Melt the butter for brushing.

7 With a little flour for dusting, roll out each portion to a 15 cm/6 in round (see pages 18–19). Lay out all the rounds in front of you and divide the filling evenly between each. Using a rubber spatula will help you to get every last little bit of the mixture out of the pan. Spread the filling out, covering the entire surface of the round. Fold all the rounds in half but don't seal them.

8 Take one of the folded rounds and use a pastry brush to brush the entire surface with butter. Pick it up to make sure both sides are brushed. Then fold the right corner to the middle, then the left corner to the middle and allow the left to overlap the right. Place it in the tin with its smooth side to the narrow end of the tin. Repeat with another two folded rounds and place them in the tin facing the same way. Repeat with a fourth folded round but turn it around and place it in the tin so

the smooth end is facing the far narrow end of the tin. Repeat with the remaining four folded rounds in the second tin. Brush the tops with any remaining melted butter.

9 Cover both tins with clingfilm (plastic wrap) and a tea towel. Allow the loaves to rise slightly for 15–30 minutes.

10 Preheat the oven to 220°C/425°F/gas 7/fan oven 200°C.

11 Bake for 24–27 minutes until well risen and dark golden brown on top.

12 Carefully turn the breads out on to a wire rack. They will tend to separate into individual portions; this is what you want but be careful while they are hot.

13 Allow the sandwiches to cool a bit before eating as the marmalade gets really hot.

14 Any leftovers can be separated and wrapped in individual portions to store in the fridge. (If you put them in the fridge as a loaf, the butter between each sandwich firms up, seals them together and then they don't come apart so well.) The sandwiches can be reheated in a preheated oven at 180°C/350°F/gas 4/fan oven 160°C for 8–9 minutes.

BREADMAKER TIPS
To make the dough, put the liquid ingredients in first, then the dry ingredients, adding the yeast last. Use the Dough programme to mix the dough and allow it to rise, then remove from the breadmaker and continue from step 4.

Hot Dog Sandwich Loaf with Mustard and Ketchup

This is a really good loaf! I love the way bits of the hot dog stick out of the bread and become almost crispy when they are baked – like they do when they have been barbecued – and the flavour is reminiscent of barbecued sausages. These are very filling and make a satisfying snack or lunch for family or friends.

MAKES 2 LOAVES

FOR THE DOUGH

500 g/1 lb 2 oz strong white bread flour

10 g/2 tsp caster (superfine) sugar

10 g/2 tsp dried milk powder (non-fat dry milk)

10 g/2 tsp salt

1 sachet + 1 tsp easy-blend dried yeast

10 g/2 tsp butter, melted

320 g/11¼ oz warm water

FOR THE FILLING

8 hot dogs (frankfurters) cooked, cooled and split in half lengthways

8 tbsp tomato ketchup (catsup)

8 generous tsp American mustard

30 g/1 oz butter, for brushing

1　Place all the dough ingredients in your mixer bowl and combine with the dough hook on speed 1 for 2 minutes or until you have soft dough that doesn't smear the bottom of the bowl. If necessary, add a little more flour or water, no more than 15 g/½ oz at a time, until you reach the desired consistency.

2　Mix on speed 2 for 10 minutes. Keep an eye on the consistency throughout; better a bit too soft than adding too much flour.

3　Take the dough out of the mixer, knead it a few times and mould it into a head (see page 14). Place the dough back in the mixing bowl, cover with clingfilm (plastic wrap) and a tea towel (dish cloth) and leave to rise for 1 hour.

4　Meanwhile, grease and flour two 450 g/1 lb 20 x 10 cm/8 x 4 in loaf tins (pans). Cook the hot dogs and split each one lengthways.

5　Divide the dough into eight 105 g/3½ oz portions and share around any leftover dough equally between the portions. Mould round (see pages 16–17), cover and allow to rest for 5 minutes. Melt the butter for brushing.

6   With a little flour for dusting, roll out each portion to a 15 cm/6 in round (see pages 18–19). Lay out all the rounds in front of you and put 1 tbsp of ketchup and a generous tsp of mustard on each. Spread the filling out, covering the entire surface of the round. Place two lengths of hot dog (one whole hot dog) cut-side up on one half of each round. Fold all the rounds in half but don't seal them.

7   Take one of the folded rounds and use a pastry brush to brush the entire surface with butter. Pick it up to make sure both sides are brushed. Then fold the right corner to the middle, then the left corner to the middle and allow the left to overlap the right. Place it in the tin with its smooth side to the narrow end of the tin. Repeat with another two folded rounds and place them in the tin facing the same way. Repeat with a fourth folded round but turn it around and place it in the tin so the smooth end is facing the far narrow end of the tin. Repeat with the remaining four rounds, arranging them in the same way in the second tin. If you have any melted butter left over, brush it over the tops of the loaves.

8   Cover both tins with clingfilm and a tea towel. Allow the loaves to rise slightly for 15–30 minutes.

9   Preheat the oven to 220°C/425°F/gas 7/fan oven 200°C.

10   Bake for 25–27 minutes until well risen and dark golden brown on top. The mustard and ketchup on top will caramelise a bit, which tastes very good!

11   Carefully turn the breads out on to a wire rack to cool.

BREADMAKER TIPS
To make the dough, put the liquid ingredients in first, then the dry ingredients, adding the yeast last. Use the Dough programme to mix the dough and allow it to rise, then remove from the breadmaker and continue from step 4.

Wholemeal Cheese and Onion Sandwich Loaf

I always try to use chopped red onion for this recipe as it has such a lovely sweet flavour and a delightful colour, too, which makes the loaf look especially good. However, if you don't have red, an ordinary white onion works just as well, so don't wait to try this delicious ploughman's-style sandwich loaf.

MAKES 2 LOAVES

FOR THE DOUGH
500 g/1 lb 2 oz wholemeal bread flour
10 g/2 tsp dark muscovado sugar
5 g/1 tsp dried milk powder (non-fat dry milk)

10 g/2 tsp salt
1 sachet + 1 tsp easy-blend dried yeast
10 g/2 tsp butter, melted
320 g/11¼ oz warm water
FOR THE FILLING
20 g/¾ oz butter

225 g/8 oz onion, finely chopped (about 3 medium onions)
Salt and freshly ground black pepper
225 g/8 oz mature Cheddar cheese, grated
5 g/1 tsp chopped fresh parsley
30 g/1 oz butter, for brushing

1   Place all the dough ingredients in your mixer bowl and combine with the dough hook on speed 1 for 2 minutes or until you have soft dough that doesn't smear the bottom of the bowl. If necessary, add a little more flour or water, no more than 15 g/½ oz at a time, until you reach the desired consistency.

2   Mix on speed 2 for 10 minutes. Keep an eye on the consistency throughout; better a bit too soft than adding too much flour.

3   Take the dough out of the mixer, knead it a few times and mould it into a head (see page 14). Place the dough back in the mixing bowl, cover with clingfilm (plastic wrap) and a tea towel (dish cloth) and leave to rise for 1 hour.

4   Meanwhile, grease and flour two 450 g/1 lb 20 x 10 cm/8 x 4 in loaf tins (pans). To prepare the filling, melt the butter in a small frying pan (skillet) over a medium heat. Add the chopped onion and cook for about 8 minutes until softened and just turning golden. Season to taste with salt and pepper and set aside to cool.

5 Divide the dough into eight 105 g/3½ oz portions and share around any leftover dough equally between the portions. Mould round (see pages 16–17), cover and allow to rest for 5 minutes. Melt the butter for brushing.

6 With a little flour for dusting, roll out each portion to a 15 cm/6 in round (see pages 18–19). Lay out all the rounds in front of you.

7 Mix the cheese and parsley into the cooled onions. Divide the filling equally between the rounds, spreading it out to cover the entire surface of the round. Fold all the rounds in half, press the edges gently but don't seal them.

8 Take one of the folded rounds and use a pastry brush to brush the entire surface with butter. Pick it up to make sure both sides are brushed. Then fold the right corner to the middle, then the left corner to the middle and allow the left to overlap the right. Place it in the tin with its smooth side to the narrow end of the tin. Repeat with another two folded rounds and place them in the tin facing the same way. Repeat with a fourth folded round but turn it around and place it in the tin so the smooth end is facing the far narrow end of the tin. Repeat with the remaining four folded rounds, arranging them in the same way in the second tin. If you have any melted butter left over, brush it over the tops of the loaves.

9 Cover both tins with clingfilm and a tea towel. Allow the loaves to rise slightly for 15–30 minutes.

10 Preheat the oven to 220°C/425°F/gas 7/fan oven 200°C.

11 Bake for 23–25 minutes until well risen and dark golden brown on top. The middle of the breads may stand up proud. Just ease them back down a little, being careful because of the steam.

12 Carefully turn the breads out on to a wire rack to cool. They will tend to separate into individual portions; this is what you want but be careful while they are hot.

13 Any leftovers can be separated and wrapped in individual portions to store in the fridge. (If you put them in the fridge as a loaf, the butter between each sandwich firms up, seals them together and then they don't come apart so well.) The sandwiches can be reheated in a preheated oven at 180°C/350°F/gas 4/fan oven 160°C for 8–9 minutes.

BREADMAKER TIPS
To make the dough, put the liquid ingredients in first, then the dry ingredients, adding the yeast last. Use the Dough programme to mix the dough and allow it to rise, then remove from the breadmaker and continue from step 4.

Hot and Spicy Mango Chutney and Cheese Sandwich Loaf

Hot and spicy mango chutney is a wonderful relish in my opinion – I think it goes well with all kinds of foods! The idea for this loaf originally came from the mango chutney and cheese toasties I used to make for lunch in those days when toasties were all the rage and developed from there.

MAKES 2 LOAVES

FOR THE DOUGH
500 g/1 lb 2 oz wholemeal bread flour
10 g/2 tsp caster (superfine) sugar

5 g/1 tsp dried milk powder (non-fat dry milk)
10 g/2 tsp salt
1 sachet + 1 tsp easy-blend dried yeast
10 g/2 tsp butter, melted
320 g/11¼ oz warm water

FOR THE FILLING
300 g/10½ oz mature Cheddar cheese, grated
120 g/4¼ oz hot and spicy mango chutney
30 g/1 oz butter, for brushing

1   Place all the dough ingredients in your mixer bowl and combine with the dough hook on speed 1 for 2 minutes or until you have soft dough that doesn't smear the bottom of the bowl. If necessary, add a little more flour or water, no more than 15 g/½ oz at a time, until you reach the desired consistency.

2   Mix on speed 2 for 10 minutes. Keep an eye on the consistency throughout; better a bit too soft than adding too much flour.

3   Take the dough out of the mixer, knead it a few times and mould it into a head (see page 14). Place the dough back in the mixing bowl, cover with clingfilm (plastic wrap) and a tea towel (dish cloth) and leave to rise for 1 hour.

4   Meanwhile, grease and flour two 450 g/1 lb 20 x 10 cm/8 x 4 in loaf tins (pans). To prepare the filling, mix the cheese into the chutney in a small bowl. Melt the butter for brushing.

5   Divide the dough into eight 105 g/3½ oz portions and share around any leftover dough equally between the portions. Mould round (see pages 16–17), cover and allow to rest for 5 minutes. Melt the butter for brushing.

6   With a little flour for dusting, roll out each round to a 15 cm/6 in round (see pages 18–19). Lay out all the rounds in front of you and divide the cheese and chutney filling equally between them. Spread it out to cover the entire surface of the round and pat it down a bit. Fold all the rounds in half but don't seal them.

7   Take one of the folded rounds and use a pastry brush to brush the entire surface with butter. Pick it up to make sure both sides are brushed. Then fold the right corner to the middle, then the left corner to the middle and allow the left to overlap the right. Place it in the tin with its smooth side to the narrow end of the tin. Repeat with another two folded rounds and place them in the tin facing the same way. Repeat with a fourth folded round but turn it around and place it in the tin so the smooth end is facing the far narrow end of the tin. Repeat with the remaining four folded rounds, arranging them in the same way in the second tin. If you have any melted butter left over, brush it over the tops of the loaves.

8   Cover both tins with clingfilm and a tea towel. Allow the loaves to rise slightly for 15–30 minutes.

9   Preheat the oven to 220°C/425°F/gas 7/fan oven 200°C.

10 Bake for 24–27 minutes until well risen and dark golden brown on top.

11 Carefully turn the breads out on to a wire rack to cool. They will tend to separate into individual portions; this is what you want but be careful while they are hot.

12 Any leftovers can be separated and wrapped in individual portions to store in the fridge. (If you put them in the fridge as a loaf, the butter between each sandwich firms up, seals them together and then they don't come apart so well.) The sandwiches can be reheated in a preheated oven at 180°C/350°F/gas 4/fan oven 160°C for 8–9 minutes.

BREADMAKER TIPS
To make the dough, put the liquid ingredients in first, then the dry ingredients, adding the yeast last. Use the Dough programme to mix the dough and allow it to rise, then remove from the breadmaker and continue from step 4.

Peanut Butter, Honey and Marshmallow Sandwich Loaf

As you can see from the title, this is a sweet sandwich loaf, which makes an unusual change. Some people like jam or jelly with their peanut butter – me included – but I think the honey and marshmallow complement the peanut butter even better. You may find it hard to stop at eating only one portion!

MAKES 2 LOAVES

FOR THE DOUGH
500 g/1 lb 2 oz strong white bread flour
20 g/³⁄₄ oz vanilla sugar

10 g/2 tsp dried milk powder (non-fat dry milk)
10 g/2 tsp salt
1 sachet + 1 tsp easy-blend dried yeast
10 g/2 tsp butter, melted
320 g/11¼ oz warm water

FOR THE FILLING
200 g/7 oz smooth or crunchy peanut butter
100 g/3½ oz clear honey
50 g/1¾ oz mini marshmallows
30 g/1 oz butter, for brushing

1 Place all the dough ingredients in your mixer bowl and combine with the dough hook on speed 1 for 2 minutes or until you have soft dough that doesn't smear the bottom of the bowl. If necessary, add a little more flour or water, no more than 15 g/½ oz at a time, until you reach the desired consistency.

2 Mix on speed 2 for 10 minutes. Keep an eye on the consistency throughout; better a bit too soft than adding too much flour.

3 Take the dough out of the mixer, knead it a few times and mould it into a head (see page 14). Place the dough back in the mixing bowl, cover with clingfilm (plastic wrap) and a tea towel (dish cloth) and leave to rise for 1 hour.

4 Divide the dough into eight 105 g/3½ oz portions and share around any leftover dough equally between the portions. Mould round (see pages 16–17), cover and allow to rest for 5 minutes. Melt the butter for brushing.

5 Meanwhile, grease and flour two 450 g/1 lb 20 x 10 cm/8 x 4 in loaf tins (pans). Warm the peanut butter until you can easily spread it (I do this carefully in the microwave), then stir in the honey.

6   With a little flour for dusting, roll out each portion to a 15 cm/6 in round (see pages 18–19). Lay out all the rounds in front of you and spoon the peanut butter and honey mixture equally between the rounds, spreading it out to cover the entire surface. You may need to warm the mixture slightly again. Share round the marshmallows, then fold all the rounds in half but don't seal them.

7   Take one of the folded rounds and use a pastry brush to brush the entire surface with butter. Pick it up to make sure both sides are brushed. Then fold the right corner to the middle, then the left corner to the middle and allow the left to overlap the right. Place it in the tin with its smooth side to the narrow end of the tin. Repeat with another two folded rounds and place them in the tin facing the same way. Repeat with a fourth folded round but turn it around and place it in the tin so the smooth end is facing the far narrow end of the tin. Repeat with the remaining four folded rounds, arranging them in the same way in the second tin. If you have any melted butter left over, brush it over the tops of the loaves.

8   Cover both tins with clingfilm and a tea towel. Allow the loaves to rise slightly for 15–30 minutes.

9   Preheat the oven to 220°C/425°F/gas 7/fan oven 200°C.

10   Bake for 24–27 minutes until well risen and dark golden brown on top.

11   Carefully turn the breads out on to a wire rack to cool.

12   Any leftovers can be reheated in a preheated oven at 180°C/350°F/gas 4/fan oven 160°C for 8–9 minutes.

BREADMAKER TIPS
To make the dough, put the liquid ingredients in first, then the dry ingredients, adding the yeast last. Use the Dough programme to mix the dough and allow it to rise, then remove from the breadmaker and continue from step 4.

Banana, Chocolate and Peanut Butter Sandwich Loaf

I'm sure you'll have heard of this combination before, even if you've never tried it. Do give it a go – you'll be surprised how good it is! I use ordinary plain chocolate for this recipe and it works well, and choose smooth or crunchy peanut butter depending on my mood! If you use a breadmaker, allow it to rise after the Dough programme, then continue from step 4.

MAKES 2 LOAVES

FOR THE DOUGH

500 g/1 lb 2 oz strong white bread flour

20 g/³⁄₄ oz caster (superfine) sugar (or light muscovado is nice)

10 g/2 tsp dried milk powder (non-fat dry milk)

10 g/2 tsp salt

1 sachet + 5 g/1 tsp easy-blend dried yeast

10 g/2 tsp butter, melted

320 g/11¹⁄₄ oz warm water

FOR THE FILLING

170 g/6 oz smooth or crunchy peanut butter

200 g/7 oz bananas (unpeeled weight)

30 g/1 oz butter, for brushing

150 g/5 oz plain (semi-sweet) chocolate chips or plain chocolate, finely chopped

1 Place all the dough ingredients in your mixer bowl and combine with the dough hook on speed 1 for 2 minutes or until you have soft, non-sticky dough. If necessary, gradually add a little more flour or water until you reach the desired consistency.

2 Mix on speed 2 for 10 minutes. Keep an eye on the consistency throughout; better a bit too soft than adding too much flour.

3 Take the dough out of the mixer, knead it a few times and mould it into a head (see page 14). Place the dough back in the mixing bowl, cover with clingfilm (plastic wrap) and a tea towel (dish cloth) and leave to rise for 1 hour.

4 Divide the dough into eight 105 g/3¹⁄₂ oz portions and share around any leftover dough equally between the portions. Mould round (see pages 16–17), cover and allow to rest for 5 minutes. Melt the butter for brushing.

5 Meanwhile, grease and flour two 450 g/1 lb 20 x 10 cm/8 x 4 in loaf tins (pans). Warm the peanut butter until you can easily spread it (I do this carefully in the microwave). Peel and slice the bananas and mash them into the peanut butter. Melt the butter for brushing.

6 With a little flour for dusting, roll out each portion to a 15 cm/6 in round (see pages 18–19). Lay out all the rounds in front of you and spoon the peanut butter and banana mixture equally

between the rounds, spreading it out to cover the entire surface of the round. Sprinkle an equal amount of the chocolate chips or chopped chocolate on the rounds, then fold them all in half but don't seal them.

7   Take one of the folded rounds and use a pastry brush to glaze the entire surface with butter. Pick it up to make sure both sides are brushed. Then fold the right corner to the middle, then the left corner to the middle and allow the left to overlap the right. Place it in the tin with its smooth side to the narrow end of the tin. Repeat with another two folded rounds and place them in the tin facing the same way. Repeat with a fourth folded round but turn it around and place it in the tin so the smooth end is facing the far narrow end of the tin. Repeat with the remaining four folded

rounds, arranging them in the same way in the second tin. If you have any melted butter left over, brush it over the tops of the loaves.

8   Cover both tins with clingfilm and a tea towel. Allow the loaves to rise slightly for 15–30 minutes.

9   Preheat the oven to 220°C/425°F/gas 7/fan oven 200°C.

10   Bake for 24–27 minutes until well risen and dark golden brown on top.

11   Carefully turn the breads out on to a wire rack to cool.

12   Any leftovers can be reheated in a preheated oven at 180°C/350°F/gas 4/fan oven 160°C for 8–9 minutes.

Bacon, Egg and Maple Syrup Sandwich Loaf

Another recipe that combines sweet and salty flavours with delicious results, the inspiration for this was a kind of cross-Atlantic breakfast: the best of a British fry-up with Canadian maple syrup, which they serve on waffles or pancakes. Pure self-indulgence!

MAKES 2 LOAVES

FOR THE DOUGH
500 g/1 lb 2 oz strong white bread flour
10 g/2 tsp caster (superfine) sugar
10 g/2 tsp dried milk powder (non-fat dry milk)

10 g/2 tsp salt
1 sachet + 5g/1 tsp easy-blend dried yeast
10 g/2 tsp butter, melted
320 g/11¼ oz warm water
FOR THE FILLING
20 g/¾ oz butter

8 rashers (slices) smoked streaky bacon, roughly chopped
6 eggs, lightly beaten
120 g/4¼ oz maple syrup
Salt and freshly ground black pepper
30 g/1 oz butter, for brushing

1   Place all the dough ingredients in your mixer bowl and combine with the dough hook on speed 1 for 2 minutes or until you have soft dough that doesn't smear the bottom of the bowl. If necessary, add a little more flour or water, no

more than 15 g/½ oz at a time, until you reach the desired consistency.

2   Mix on speed 2 for 10 minutes. Keep an eye on the consistency throughout; better a bit too soft than adding too much flour.

3   Take the dough out of the mixer, knead it a few times and mould it into a head (see page 14). Place the dough back in the mixing bowl, cover with clingfilm (plastic wrap) and a tea towel (dish cloth) and leave to rise for 1 hour.

4   Meanwhile, grease and flour two 450 g/1 lb 20 x 10 cm/8 x 4 in loaf tins (pans).

5   To prepare the filling, melt the butter in a small frying pan (skillet) and fry (sauté) the bacon over a medium heat for 2–3 minutes. Add the eggs and cook for about 2–3 minutes until they are scrambled but not overly dry. Add the maple syrup, season to taste and set aside to cool.

6   Divide the dough into eight 105 g/3½ oz portions and share around any leftover dough equally between the portions. Mould round (see pages 16–17), cover and allow to rest for 10 minutes. Melt the butter for brushing.

7   With a little flour for dusting, roll out each portion to a 15 cm/6 in round (see pages 18–19). Spread the filling evenly over the surfaces. Fold the rounds in half but don't seal them.

8   Brush both sides of one round with the butter. Fold the right corner to the middle, then the left corner to the middle and allow the left to overlap the right. Place it in the tin with its smooth side to the narrow end of the tin. Repeat with another two folded rounds. Repeat with a fourth folded round but turn it around and place it in the tin so the smooth end is facing the far narrow end of the tin. Repeat with the remaining four folded

rounds in the second tin. Brush the tops with any remaining melted butter.

9   Cover the pans with clingfilm and a tea towel and allow to rise for 15–30 minutes. Preheat the oven to 220°C/425°F/gas 7/fan oven 200°C.

10 Bake for 24–27 minutes until well risen and dark golden brown on top.

11 Carefully turn the breads out on to a wire rack. They will tend to separate into portions; this is what you want but be careful while they are hot.

12 Separate any leftovers, wrap and store in the fridge. The sandwiches can be reheated in a preheated oven at 180°C/350°F/gas 4/fan oven 160°C for 8–9 minutes.

BREADMAKER TIPS
To make the dough, put the liquid ingredients in first, then the dry ingredients, adding the yeast last. Use the Dough programme to mix the dough and allow it to rise, then remove from the breadmaker and continue from step 4.

FANCY LOAVES

I like to think that if you saw these loaves in a shop, you would say 'Oooh! What's that?' and have to go and take a closer look and then really want to try them! Each of the breads has a jewel-like quality about it, most are multi-faceted in their construction with fruit and nuts adding sparks of interest. Don't be put off! These fancy loaves are very easy to make and really satisfying, too, when you get brilliant results. Your metal dough scraper will be invaluable here for chopping in all the delicious filling ingredients.

Ginger, Ginger, Gingerbread

All the rough peaks in this delicious loaf turn a lovely golden colour once baked, and the bread isn't overly sweet, so it appeals to adults just as much as to children. I think it makes really good breakfast bread. Heat up a chunk in the oven so you have nice crusty bits on top and a warm, soft inside.

MAKES 2 LOAVES

FOR THE DOUGH
500 g/1 lb 2 oz strong white bread flour
5 g/1 tsp salt
10 g/2 tsp caster (superfine) sugar

5 g/1 tsp ground ginger
1 sachet of easy-blend dried yeast
30 g/1 oz oil
300 g/10½ oz ginger beer warmed to
  36°C/97°F

FOR THE FILLING
80 g/2¾ oz stem ginger (about 5 balls)
FOR THE TOPPING
10 g/2 tsp oil
30 g/1 oz stem ginger syrup, from the jar

1   Place all the dough ingredients in your mixer bowl and combine with the dough hook on speed 1 for 2 minutes or until you have soft dough that doesn't smear the bottom of the bowl. You may need to add a little warm water, no more than 15 g/½ oz at a time, to get the desired consistency.

2   Mix on speed 2 for 10 minutes. Add a little flour, no more than 15 g/½ oz at a time, if necessary to maintain a soft but not smeary dough.

3   Mould the dough into a head (see page 14), cover with clingfilm (plastic wrap) and a tea towel (dish cloth) and leave to rise for 30 minutes.

4   Uncover and punch down the dough, mould it back into a head, then re-cover and allow to rise for another 30 minutes (it won't rise a great deal).

5   Meanwhile, chop the stem ginger into fairly small dice. Mix together the oil and stem ginger syrup in a small bowl or ramekin (custard cup). Grease and flour two baking (cookie) sheets, at least 30 x 23 cm/12 x 9 in, or line with a non–stick liner.

6 Take the dough out of the mixing bowl and press it out into a rough round about 2.5 cm/1 in thick on top of your work surface. Spread the diced ginger all over the top, then fold the dough in on itself to encase the cubes.

7 Using your metal scraper, chop right through the dough until it is in rough pieces about 5 cm/2 in thick (see page 23). Mound up the pieces, twisting and turning them so the ginger chunks mix in. Don't press them together into a solid lump!

8 Repeat the chopping until the ginger is evenly mixed in; it usually takes four or five goes to distribute the ginger throughout the dough. Again, don't press the dough into a solid lump.

9 Give the ginger syrup mixture a quick whisk with a fork, then pour the mixture all over your rough heap of dough.

10 Using your metal scraper, chop the ginger syrup and oil mixture into the dough, making smaller pieces this time (about 2.5 cm/1 in wide is good, but don't worry too much as it is meant to be rough). Make sure the syrup is distributed throughout the dough, but stop before the dough absorbs all the mixture.

11 Divide the dough into two equal mounds, each weighing about 450 g/1 lb. Take one of the mounds and pile it up in a fairly even, flattish, 15 cm/6 in round in the centre of one of the baking sheets. Add in any escaped bits of stem ginger. Repeat for the other mound.

12 Cover both gently and loosely with clingfilm and a tea towel and allow to rise for about 30 minutes until puffy.

13 About 15 minutes before the end of the rising time, preheat the oven to 220°C/425°F/gas 7/fan oven 200°C.

14 Bake the loaves, one at a time, for 13–15 minutes until the rough tips of the loaves are dark golden. Don't over-bake – you want this to be a soft bread.

15 Transfer the breads to a wire rack to cool.

BREADMAKER TIPS

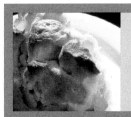

To make the dough, put the liquid ingredients in first, then the dry ingredients, adding the yeast last. Either bake one large loaf using the Basic programme, adding the filling ingredients after the first rising, or use the Dough programme to mix the dough and allow it to rise, then remove from the breadmaker and continue from step 5.

Buttery, Honey and Nut Loaf

I don't think you can beat toasted nuts for their wonderful flavour and texture, so here is a little bread, butter and honey to go with them. You can use a mixture of whole nuts – perhaps pecans, cashews and almonds – or just one type, if you prefer, so there are plenty of variations on a theme and no excuse if you can't buy one type!

MAKES 1 LOAF

FOR THE DOUGH
280 g/10 oz strong white bread flour
25 g/1 oz vanilla sugar
1/2 tsp salt
10 g/2 tsp dried milk powder (non-fat dry milk)

1 sachet of easy-blend dried yeast
1/4 tsp ground ginger
1/2 tsp ground cinnamon
15 g/1/2 oz butter, melted
1 egg, beaten
1/2 tsp vanilla essence (extract)
100 g/31/2 oz warm water

FOR THE FILLING
150 g/5 oz whole nuts
20 g/3/4 oz butter
1/2 tsp vanilla essence (extract)
FOR THE TOPPING
50 g/13/4 oz clear honey

1   Place all the dough ingredients in your mixer bowl and combine with the dough hook on speed 1 for 2 minutes or until you have soft dough that doesn't smear the bottom of the bowl. You may need to add a little warm water, no more than 15 g/1/2 oz at a time, to reach the very soft dough you need.

2   Mix on speed 2 for 10 minutes, maintaining a soft but not smeary dough. If the dough starts smearing on the bottom of the bowl during this stage, add a little bread flour, no more than 15 g/ 1/2 oz at a time, to maintain this soft texture.

3   Mould the dough into a head (see page 14), cover with clingfilm (plastic wrap) and a tea towel (dish cloth) and leave to rise for 30 minutes.

4   Uncover and punch down the dough, knead it a bit and shape it back into a head. Re-cover the dough and allow to rise for another 30 minutes.

5   Meanwhile, grease and flour a baking (cookie) sheet, at least 30 x 23 cm/12 x 9 in, or just line with non-stick liner. Toast the nuts all together

for 10–12 minutes in a preheated oven at 180°C/350°F/gas 4/fan oven 160°C. Melt the butter and add the vanilla essence when it has cooled a little.

6 Take the dough out of the mixing bowl and press it out into a rough round about 2.5 cm/1 in thick on top of your work surface. Pile the nuts on top of the dough, then fold the dough in on itself to encase the them.

7 Using your metal scraper, chop right through the dough until the nuts look evenly distributed throughout (see page 23). Mound up the pieces, but don't press them together into a solid lump.

8 Pour the melted butter and vanilla mixture all over the dough.

9 Using your metal scraper, chop through the dough again until the butter mixture is distributed evenly, but stop before the dough starts to absorb the butter.

10 Pile the dough into a fairly even, flattish 20 cm/ 8 in round on the centre of the baking sheet. Add in any escaped nuts.

11 Cover gently and loosely with clingfilm and a tea towel and allow the bread to rise for about 45 minutes until puffy.

12 About 15 minutes before the end of the rising time, preheat the oven to 220°C/425°F/gas 7/fan oven 200°C.

13 Bake the loaf for 20–22 minutes until a dark golden colour.

14 Transfer to a wire rack. Warm the honey slightly, then brush it all over the loaf.

BREADMAKER TIPS
To make the dough, put the liquid ingredients in first, then the dry ingredients, adding the yeast last. Either bake the loaf using the Basic programme, adding the filling ingredients after the first rising, or use the Dough programme to mix the dough and allow it to rise, then remove from the breadmaker and continue from step 5.

Inspired Rhubarb, Apple and Sultana Bread

The inspiration for this was a pie I cobbled together one Sunday and served with custard. I haven't sweetened the fruit because the dough is sweet and the demerara topping adds sweetness and crunch. This way, some bites of fruit are sweet and some are still a bit tart. This bread is wonderful warm from the oven.

MAKES 1 LOAF

FOR THE DOUGH
290 g/10¼ oz strong white bread flour
25 g/1 oz light muscovado sugar
½ tsp salt
10 g/2 tsp dried milk powder (non-fat dry milk)
¼ tsp ground ginger

5 g/1 tsp ground cinnamon
1 sachet of easy-blend dried yeast
15 g/½ oz butter, melted
1 egg, beaten
½ tsp vanilla essence (extract)
100 g/3½ oz warm water

FOR THE FILLING
30 g/1 oz sultanas (golden raisins)

70 g/2½ oz rhubarb, chopped to about sultana size
1 unpeeled eating (dessert) apple (about 100 g/3½ oz), cored and quartered
20 g/¾ oz butter
½ tsp vanilla essence (extract)

FOR THE TOPPING
40 g/1½ oz demerara sugar

1 Place all the dough ingredients in your mixer bowl and combine with the dough hook on speed 1 for 2 minutes or until you have soft dough that doesn't smear the bottom of the bowl. You may need to add a little warm water, no more than 15 g/½ oz at a time, to reach the very soft dough you need.

2 Mix on speed 2 for 10 minutes. If the dough is only slightly smearing on the bottom of the mixer, let it stay that way; it should absorb towards the end of the 10 minutes.

3 Take the dough out of the mixer, knead it a few times and mould it into a head (see page 14). Place it back in the mixing bowl, cover with clingfilm (plastic wrap) and a tea towel (dish cloth) and leave to rise for 30 minutes.

4 Uncover and punch down the dough, knead it a bit and shape it back into a head. Re-cover the dough and allow to rise for another 30 minutes.

5 Meanwhile, grease and flour a baking (cookie) sheet, at least 30 x 23 cm/12 x 9 in, or just line

with non-stick liner. Alternatively, grease and flour a 20 cm/8 in pie tin (pan) and place it on a baking sheet.

6 Mix together the fruits. Melt the butter and add the vanilla essence when it has cooled a little.

7 Take the dough out of the mixing bowl and press it out into a rough round about 2.5 cm/1 in thick on top of your work surface. Pile the fruit filling on top of the dough, then fold the dough in on itself to encase the filling – lots of fruit will fall out but don't worry.

8 Using your metal scraper, chop right through the dough into rough pieces about 5 cm/2 in thick until the nuts look evenly distributed throughout (see page 23). Mound up the pieces, twisting and turning them so the fruits mix in. There is a lot of fruit but repeat until it looks evenly distributed. Don't press everything together into a solid lump.

9 Pour the melted butter and vanilla mixture all over the bread. Chop all the way through the mound of dough again until the mixture is distributed evenly, but stop before the dough starts to absorb the butter.

10 Pile up all the bits of dough and fruit into a neat 18 cm/7 in pile on the prepared baking sheet – don't press it all together. If you are using a pie tin, just place the dough and fruits loosely in the tin and return the tin to the baking sheet.

11 Cover loosely with clingfilm and a tea towel and allow to rise for 45 minutes.

12 About 15 minutes before the end of the rising time, preheat the oven to 220°C/425°F/gas 7/fan oven 200°C. Sprinkle the demerara sugar evenly over the bread.

13 Bake the loaf for 20–25 minutes until a deep golden colour. Don't panic if the bread is quite dark in colour; it's just the sugar in the dough and on top.

14 Transfer to a wire rack to cool.

BREADMAKER TIPS
To make the dough, put the liquid ingredients in first, then the dry ingredients, adding the yeast last. Either bake the loaf using the Basic programme, adding the filling ingredients after the first rising, or use the Dough programme to mix the dough and allow it to rise, then remove from the breadmaker and continue from step 5.

Rum and Raisin Choppy Loaf

I got to thinking about the custardy flavour of Inspired Rhubarb, Apple and Sultana Bread (see page 62) and thought: 'Well, that's not too far away from ice cream, and rum 'n' raisin ice cream is delicious. I wonder if it would work as a bread ...' So I had a go and was pleased with the results. I think you will be, too!

MAKES 1 LOAF

FOR THE DOUGH
290 g/10¼ oz strong white bread flour
30 g/1 oz caster (superfine) sugar
½ tsp salt

10 g/2 tsp dried milk powder (non-fat dry milk)
1 sachet of easy-blend dried yeast
15 g/½ oz butter, melted
1 egg, beaten
5 g/1 tsp vanilla essence (extract)
100 g/3½ oz warm water

FOR THE FILLING
100 g/3½ oz raisins
70 g/2½ oz rum
20 g/¾ oz butter
½ tsp vanilla essence
FOR THE TOPPING
40 g/1½ oz demerara sugar

1   Soak the raisins for the filling in the rum for at least 1 hour, preferably overnight.

2   Place all the dough ingredients in your mixer bowl and combine with the dough hook on speed 1 for 2 minutes or until you have soft dough that doesn't smear the bottom of the bowl. You may need to add a little warm water, no more than 15 g/½ oz at a time, to reach the very soft dough you need.

3   Mix on speed 2 for 10 minutes, maintaining a soft but not smeary dough. If it does start smearing the bottom of the bowl, add a little bread flour, no more than 15 g/½ oz at a time, to get the desired consistency.

4   Take the dough out of the mixer, knead it a few times and mould it into a head (see page 14). Place it back in the mixing bowl, cover with clingfilm (plastic wrap) and a tea towel (dish cloth) and leave to rise for 1 hour.

5   Meanwhile, grease and flour a 20 cm/8 in round cake tin (pan) or pie tin and place the tin on a baking (cookie) sheet. (You could also use a 30 x 23 cm/12 x 9 in baking sheet, greased and

floured or lined with non-stick liner, and just pile the dough and fruit on it in a neat 18 cm/7 in pile at step 9.) Melt the butter and drain the raisins, pouring the rum into the melted butter. Add the vanilla essence.

6 Take the dough out of the mixing bowl and press it out into a rough round about 2.5 cm/1 in thick on top of your work surface. Pile the soaked raisins on top of the dough, then fold the dough in on itself to encase them – lots of the raisins will fall out but don't worry.

7 Using your metal scraper, chop right through the dough into rough pieces about 5 cm/2 in thick until the raisins look evenly distributed throughout (see page 23). Mound up the pieces, twisting and turning them so the raisins mix in. Don't press everything together into a solid lump.

8 Pour the melted butter, vanilla and rum mixture all over the dough. Chop all the way through the mound of dough again until the mixture is distributed evenly, but stop before the dough starts to absorb the butter. It will be very wet; don't get scared!

9 Pile up all the bits of dough and raisins evenly into the prepared cake tin or pie tin. Don't press it all together; just mound it up loosely.

10 Cover loosely with clingfilm and a tea towel and allow to rise for 45 minutes.

11 About 15 minutes before the end of the rising time, preheat the oven to 220°C/425°F/gas 7/fan oven 200°C. Sprinkle the demerara sugar evenly over the bread.

12 Bake the loaf for 20–23 minutes until a dark golden colour.

13 Transfer to a wire rack to cool. (You will probably need to loosen the bread from the sides of the tin with a butter knife.)

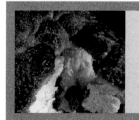

BREADMAKER TIPS
To make the dough, put the liquid ingredients in first, then the dry ingredients, adding the yeast last. Either bake the loaf using the Basic programme, adding the filling ingredients after the first rising, or use the Dough programme to mix the dough and allow it to rise, then remove from the breadmaker and continue from step 5.

Parsnip, Honey and Brown Sugar Bread

I love the combination of sweet and savoury! I have served this alongside a thick, creamy potato soup, which everyone thoroughly enjoyed, but you can serve it with any soups or just on its own. In a breadmaker, you can use the Basic programme, adding the filling after the first rising; or the Dough programme, continuing from step 4.

MAKES 1 LOAF

FOR THE DOUGH
250 g/9 oz strong white bread flour
5 g/1 tsp salt
5 g/1 tsp dried milk powder (non-fat dry milk)
1 sachet of easy-blend dried yeast
10 g/2 tsp honey
25 g/1 oz butter, melted
135 g/4³/₄ oz warm water

FOR THE TOPPING
200 g/7 oz peeled and grated parsnip
40 g/1¹/₂ oz light muscovado sugar
Salt and freshly ground black pepper
30 g/1 oz butter, melted
50 g/1³/₄ oz clear honey

1   Place all the dough ingredients in your mixer bowl and combine with the dough hook on speed 1 for 2 minutes or until you have soft dough that doesn't smear the bottom of the bowl. Add a little flour or warm water, 15 g/¹/₂ oz at a time, if necessary to get the desired consistency.

2   Mix on speed 2 for 10 minutes, maintaining a soft but not smeary dough. If necessary, add a little flour, no more than 15 g/¹/₂ oz at a time.

3   Take the dough out of the mixer, knead it a few times and mould it into a head (see page 14). Place it back in the mixing bowl, cover with clingfilm (plastic wrap) and a tea towel (dish cloth) and leave to rise for 1 hour or until doubled in size.

4   Take the dough out of the mixing bowl, mould it back into a head, re-cover and allow to rest for 10 minutes.

5   Meanwhile, grease and flour a 28 x 18 cm/11 x 7 in baking (cookie) sheet or just line with non-stick liner. Mix together the parsnip, sugar and a little salt and pepper.

6   Using a rolling pin, roll out the dough to a 30 x 20 in/12 x 8 in rectangle (see pages 21–22). Use white bread flour for dusting. Place the rectangle on the prepared baking tin and ease the dough up against the sides of the tin. Brush the top edges and sides of the dough with a little melted butter. Add any remaining butter to the parsnips.

7   Spread the filling evenly over the base of the dough and drizzle with the honey.

8   Cover with clingfilm and a tea towel and allow to rise for 20 minutes. Preheat the oven to 200°C/400°F/gas 6/fan oven 180°C.

9   Bake for 18–20 minutes until golden.

10 Transfer to a wire rack to cool.

ROLLS AND BUNS

Here is a mixture of sweet and savoury rolls and buns. They can be split and toasted or they can be eaten on their own. They are wonderful with or without a filling.

When you are making them I highly recommend portioning the dough accurately by weight, rather than guessing by eye. You will then be sure that all of your buns bake evenly.

To portion the dough, use your metal dough scraper and chop off a lump of about the weight you think you want. Place the lump on your scales then add or take away dough to get the weight you want.

When you have the correct number of buns, any extra dough can be shared equally around the portions. You will quickly get an eye for how much dough you need for each portion and before long you'll be whizzing through this stage.

Double Knots

These look very professional and impressive but are actually really easy to make. Even if you find shaping them a bit tricky to start with, you'll soon get the hang of it after the first one or two. With the light egg wash, the rolls turn out a beautiful golden colour. Their texture is light and they taste perfectly delicious.

MAKES 10 ROLLS

FOR THE DOUGH
560 g/1 lb 3¹/₂ oz strong white bread flour
10 g/2 tsp caster (superfine) sugar

10 g/2 tsp salt
10 g/2 tsp dried milk powder (non-fat dry milk)
1 sachet of easy-blend dried yeast
50 g/1³/₄ oz unsalted butter, melted

300 g/10¹/₂ oz warm water
FOR THE EGG WASH
1 egg yolk mixed with 15 g/¹/₂ oz water

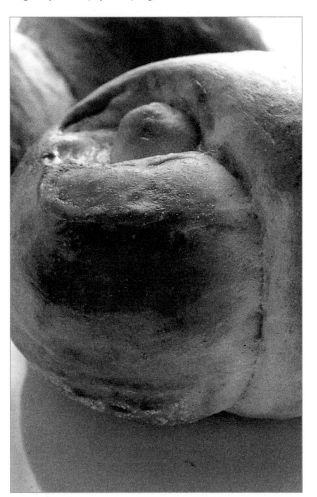

1. Place all the dough ingredients in your mixer bowl and combine with the dough hook on speed 1 for 2 minutes until you have a soft dough that doesn't smear the bottom of the bowl. You may need to add a little warm water, no more than 15 g/¹/₂ oz at a time, to get the desired consistency.

2. Mix on speed 2 for 10 minutes. Keep an eye on the consistency throughout; better a bit too soft than adding too much flour.

3. Take the dough out of the mixer, knead it a few times and mould it into a head (see page 14). Place it back in the mixing bowl, cover with clingfilm (plastic wrap) and a tea towel (dish cloth) and leave to rise for 1 hour.

4. Knock the dough back, knead it a few times and reshape it into a head. Re-cover the dough and leave to rise for a further hour.

5. Meanwhile, grease and flour two large baking (cookie) sheets or just line with non-stick liner.

6. Gently punch the dough down, then take it out of the mixer. Divide it into ten 90 g/3 oz portions and share around any leftover dough equally between the portions. Mould the portions round (see pages 16–17), cover and leave to rest for 15 minutes.

7 Roll out each portion into a 40 cm/16 in sausage (see page 20). You shouldn't need any extra flour for the rolling as the dough isn't sticky.

8 Have a small pile of flour off to the side of your work surface. Take each sausage to this pile and give it a very light dusting of flour.

9 To make a knot, lay a sausage horizontally in front of you. Bring both ends to the centre of the sausage, place the ends side by side and lay them over the sausage, away from you, to extend about 4 cm/1½ inches beyond the horizontal line of the sausage. Tuck the end of one sausage up through a loop. The very end of the sausage will now poke up through and fill the loop. Repeat on the other side. Repeat with the remaining dough sausages, then cover with clingfilm and a tea towel and allow to rise for 30 minutes.

10 Preheat the oven to 220°C/425°F/gas 7/fan oven 200°C.

11 Brush the buns all over with the egg wash, being careful to brush them as evenly as possible because missed spots really show up! (If it took you a little while to shape all the knots and the second sheet hasn't risen as quickly as the first, just bake those on the first sheet and allow the second to finish rising.)

12 Bake for 12–15 minutes until golden.

13 Transfer to a wire rack to cool a little. Serve warm.

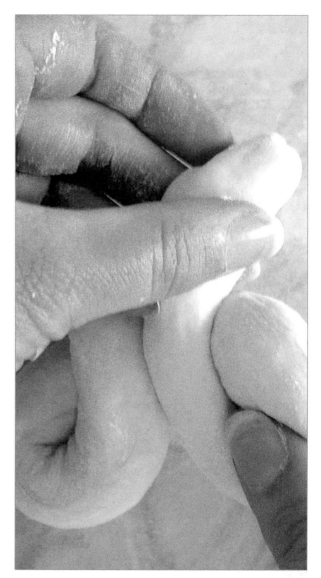

BREADMAKER TIPS
To make the dough, put the liquid ingredients in first, then the dry ingredients, adding the yeast last. Use the Dough programme to mix the dough and allow it to rise, then remove from the breadmaker and continue from step 4.

Bagels

A newly baked bagel has a shiny, crisp crust and is warm and chewy inside because it is boiled, then baked. I like the boiling stage; it's fun to watch the bagels expanding. The dough needs to be quite stiff, so it will feel less soft than other dough but don't get it too stiff or your mixer won't cope!

MAKES 12 BAGELS

FOR THE DOUGH
625 g/1 lb 6 oz strong white bread flour

15 g/¹⁄₂ oz salt
25 g/1 oz honey
1 sachet of easy-blend dried yeast
15 g/¹⁄₂ oz oil

330 g/11¹⁄₂ oz warm water
FOR BOILING
40 g/1¹⁄₂ oz granulated sugar

1 Place all the dough ingredients in your mixer bowl and combine with the dough hook on speed 1 for 2 minutes until you have a fairly stiff dough that doesn't smear the bottom of the bowl.

2 Mix on speed 2 for 10 minutes.

3 Take the dough out of the mixer, knead it a few times and mould it into a head (see page 14). Place it back in the mixing bowl, cover with clingfilm (plastic wrap) and a tea towel (dish cloth) and leave to rise for 1¹⁄₂ hours.

4 Gently punch the dough down, then take it out of the mixer. Divide it into twelve 80 g/2³⁄₄ oz portions and share around any leftover dough equally between the portions. Mould the portions round (see pages 16–17). Bagel dough dries out very quickly, so keep the dough you are not working with covered while you mould round. You may also need to lightly spritz the dough or your work surface with water to prevent the dough from slipping while you are moulding round.

5 Allow the portions to rest, still covered, for 15 minutes. Meanwhile, grease and flour two large baking (cookie) sheets or just line with non-stick liner. Put the sugar and about 2¹⁄₂ litres/4¹⁄₂ pints of water in a large saucepan ready to bring to the boil.

6   Roll each portion into a 20 cm/8 in sausage (see page 20), then shape into a ring by overlapping one end on top of the other and pinching the ends together very firmly. Bend and twist the pinched dough around itself to really mangle the ends together so there is no chance of them coming apart. Remember to keep both the completed rings and the portions you haven't worked on yet covered.

7   Place six bagels on each baking sheet and cover each with clingfilm and a tea towel. Leave to rise for 45 minutes.

8   About 20 minutes before the end of the rising time, bring the pan of water to the boil. The sugar gives the bagels colour and the boiling makes them chewy. Preheat the oven to 240°C/475°F/ gas 9/fan oven 215°C.

9   Now the fun bit! Carefully lift a bagel off one of the sheets (it will be pretty sturdy but you do need to be a bit gentle) and slide it into the boiling water. Add two more bagels and then let them all boil for 30 seconds. Turn the bagels over with a slotted spoon and give them another 30 seconds. A timer is useful – your attention can wander far away in 30 seconds!

10 Using the slotted spoon, carefully lift out each bagel and place it back on the baking sheet. Repeat the whole process until you have boiled all the bagels.

11 Place the sheets in the preheated oven and bake the bagels for 12–15 minutes or until they are well risen, golden and sound hollow when you tap on their bases. I usually find that about 3 minutes before the end of the baking time I need to turn the sheets round in the oven so all the bagels colour evenly.

12 Transfer to a wire rack to cool a little before eating. Any left over should be frozen as soon as they are cold as they go stale very quickly.

BREADMAKER TIPS
To make the dough, put the liquid ingredients in first, then the dry ingredients, adding the yeast last. You may need to add 15–30 ml/1–2 tbsp more water to knead in all the flour. Use the Dough programme to mix the dough and allow it to rise. Leave it in the breadmaker for an extra 30 minutes to continue to rise, then remove from the breadmaker and continue from step 4.

Cinnamon and Raisin Bagels

These are dedicated to Dot and Howard Greville, who helped us find and look after our Doberman puppy, Piper. Thirteen is often called a 'baker's dozen'. It is said to originate from the fact that bakers in the thirteenth century used to add an extra loaf to every 12 rather than risk the penalties associated with short orders!

MAKES 13 BAGELS

FOR THE DOUGH
610 g/1 lb 5½ oz strong white bread flour
15 g/½ oz ground cinnamon

15 g/½ oz salt
50 g/1¾ oz light muscovado sugar
1 sachet of easy-blend dried yeast
55 g/scant 2 oz honey
15 g/½ oz oil

310 g/11 oz warm water
FOR THE FILLING
120 g/4¼ oz raisins
FOR BOILING
40 g/1½ oz granulated sugar

1. Place all the dough ingredients in your mixer bowl and combine with the dough hook on speed 1 for 2 minutes until you have a fairly stiff dough that doesn't smear the bottom of the bowl.

2. Mix on speed 2 for 10 minutes.

3. Take the dough out of the mixer, knead it a few times and mould it into a head (see page 14). Place it back in the mixing bowl, cover with clingfilm (plastic wrap) and a tea towel (dish cloth) and leave to rise for 1½ hours.

4. Gently punch the dough down, take it out of the mixer and lay it out on your work surface. Pat it out until it is about 2.5 cm/1 in thick. Lay the raisins on top and bring the sides of the dough up to encase the filling.

5. Using your metal scraper, chop the raisins into the dough until they are evenly distributed (see page 23).

6. Gently punch the dough down, then take it out of the mixer. Divide it into thirteen 90 g/3 oz portions and share around any leftover dough equally between the portions. Mould the portions round (see pages 16–17). Bagel dough dries out very quickly, so keep the dough you are not

working with covered while you mould round. You may also need to lightly spritz the dough or your work surface with water to prevent the dough from slipping while you are moulding round.

7 Allow the portions to rest, still covered, for 15 minutes. Meanwhile, grease and flour two large baking (cookie) sheets or just line with non-stick liner. Put the sugar and about 2½ litres/4½ pints of water in a large saucepan ready to bring to the boil.

8 Roll each portion into a 20 cm/8 in sausage (see page 20), then shape into a ring by overlapping one end on top of the other and pinching the ends together very firmly. Bend and twist the pinched dough around itself to really mangle the ends together so there is no chance of them coming apart. Remember to keep both the completed rings and the portions you haven't worked on yet covered.

9 Place six bagels on each baking sheet and cover each with clingfilm and a tea towel. Leave to rise for 45–60 minutes.

10 About 20 minutes before the end of the rising time, bring the pan of water to the boil. The sugar gives the bagels colour and the boiling makes them chewy. Preheat the oven to 240°C/475°F/gas 9/fan oven 215°C.

11 Now the fun bit! Carefully lift a bagel off one of the sheets (it will be pretty sturdy but you do need to be a bit gentle) and slide it into the boiling water. Add two more bagels and then let them all boil for 30 seconds. Turn the bagels over with a slotted spoon and give them another 30 seconds. A timer is useful – your attention can wander far away in 30 seconds!

12 Using the slotted spoon, carefully lift out each bagel and place it back on to the baking sheet. Repeat the whole process until you have boiled all the bagels.

13 Place the sheets in the preheated oven and bake the bagels for 12–14 minutes or until they are well risen, golden and sound hollow when you tap on their bases. I usually find that about 3 minutes before the end of the baking time I need to turn the sheets around in the oven so all the bagels colour evenly.

14 Transfer to a wire rack to cool a little before eating. Any left over should be frozen as soon as they are cold as they go stale very quickly.

BREADMAKER TIPS

To make the dough, put the liquid ingredients in first, then the dry ingredients, adding the yeast last. Use the Dough programme to mix the dough and allow it to rise. Leave it in the breadmaker for an extra 30 minutes to continue to rise, then remove from the breadmaker and continue from step 4.

Bialys

Pronounced 'bee-ah-lees', these are my take on the little breads that come from Bialystock in Poland. I love them – especially for lunch! I have read that the best way to eat a bialy is hot, with cream cheese or butter smeared over the top. Quite possibly true, but I also know they make a fantastic tuna sandwich.

MAKES 8 ROLLS

FOR THE DOUGH
425 g/15 oz strong white bread flour
1 sachet of easy-blend dried yeast

6 g/1¼ tsp salt
260 g/9¼ oz warm water
FOR THE FILLING
160 g/5½ oz white onion (peeled and
   trimmed weight)

20 g/¾ oz olive oil
5 g/1 tsp poppy seeds

1. Place the dough ingredients in your mixer bowl and combine with the dough hook on speed 1 for 2 minutes until you have a soft, smooth dough. You may need to add a little flour or warm water, no more than 15 g/½ oz at a time, to get the desired consistency.

2. Mix on speed 2 for 10 minutes, adding flour or warm water as needed to maintain a soft but not smeary dough.

3. Take the dough out of the mixer, knead it a few times and mould it into a head (see page 14). Place it back in the mixing bowl, cover with clingfilm (plastic wrap) and a tea towel (dish cloth) and leave to rise for 30 minutes.

4. Punch the dough down, mould it back into a head, re-cover and leave to rise again for 1 hour or until doubled in size.

5. Meanwhile, grease and flour two large baking (cookie) sheets or just line with non-stick liner.

6. Divide the dough into eight 80 g/2¾ oz portions and share around any leftover dough equally between the portions. Mould the portions round (see pages 16–17), cover and allow to rest for 5 minutes.

7   Using some flour for dusting, roll each portion into a 10 cm/4 in round (see pages 18–19). Place all the rounds on your baking sheets.

8   Cover each sheet with clingfilm and a tea towel and leave the dough to rise for 30 minutes while you prepare the filling.

9   Halve the onion through the root, then slice each half thinly. Heat the olive oil in a small frying pan (skillet), add the onion and fry (sauté) for 3–4 minutes until softened. Remove the pan from the heat, add the poppy seeds, mix thoroughly and transfer the filling to a bowl to cool. Stir the filling from time to time to help it cool evenly. You can use scissors to chop the mixture in the bowl if you don't like long pieces of onion.

10 When the rounds have fully risen, dust the end of your rolling pin or a small glass (I use the bottom of a pudding basin) with flour and press it firmly into the middle of each round. Press until you are flat against the bottom of your baking sheet. Take a fork and press it a few times in the indentation – this will help to keep the centre flat. All the rounds should have a deep indentation in the middle surrounded by a ring of thick dough.

11 Preheat the oven to 240°C/475°F/gas 9/fan oven 215°C. Spoon the filling equally into each of the indentations. Lightly dust the outer ring with flour.

12 Bake for 9–10 minutes until pale golden.

13 Transfer to a wire rack to cool a little, then serve while still warm. Bialys go stale quickly but freeze and reheat very well, so any left over should be frozen as soon as they are cold.

BREADMAKER TIPS
To make the dough, put the liquid ingredients in first, then the dry ingredients, adding the yeast last. Use the Dough programme to mix the dough and allow it to rise. Leave it in the breadmaker for an extra 30 minutes to continue to rise, then remove from the breadmaker and continue from step 5.

German-inspired Muesli Rolls

I spent some time in Germany at Rischart's Bakery in Munich, working in all areas – konditorei, backerei, confiserie, feinbackerei – even though I knew no German! For breakfast, we had a choice of different rolls each morning, but I was hooked by the muesli brot rolls, which I drenched with honey and enjoyed with my coffee.

MAKES 15 ROLLS

FOR THE DOUGH
700 g/1 lb 9 oz strong white bread flour
70 g/2¹/₂ oz porridge oats
15 g/¹/₂ oz salt
20 g/¹/₂ oz light muscovado sugar

10 g/2 tsp dried milk powder (non-fat dry milk)
1 sachet of easy-blend dried yeast
30 g/1 oz butter, melted
50 g/1³/₄ oz honey
1 egg, beaten
380 g/13¹/₂ oz warm water

FOR THE FILLING
50 g/1³/₄ oz whole almonds
50 g/1³/₄ oz whole hazelnuts (filberts)
50 g/1³/₄ oz sultanas (golden raisins)

FOR THE TOPPING
130 g/4¹/₂ oz clear honey
140 g/5 oz jumbo oats

1   Place all the dough ingredients in your mixer bowl and combine with the dough hook on speed 1 for 2 minutes until you have a soft dough that doesn't smear the bottom of the bowl. You may need to add a little flour or warm water, no more than 15 g/¹/₂ oz at a time, to get the desired consistency.

2   Mix on speed 2 for 10 minutes, adding flour or water as needed to maintain the correct consistency.

3   Take the dough out of the mixer, knead it a few times and mould it into a head (see page 14). Place it back in the mixing bowl, cover with clingfilm (plastic wrap) and a tea towel (dish cloth) and leave to rise for 1¹/₂ hours or until doubled in size.

4   Meanwhile, grease and flour two large baking (cookie) sheets or just line with non-stick liner. Preheat the oven to 180°C/350°F/gas 4/fan oven 160°C. Place the whole almonds and hazelnuts on a third baking sheet and toast for 7–8 minutes in the preheated oven. Turn off the oven. Combine the nuts with the sultanas in a small bowl.

5 Take the dough out of the mixer, flatten it out a bit on the work surface and spread the filling on top of the dough. Fold the dough over the fruits to enclose them, then use a metal scraper to cut the fruit and chocolate into the dough (see page 23).

6 Divide the dough into fifteen 80 g/2¾ oz portions and share around any leftover dough equally between the portions. Mould the portions round (see pages 16–17) and place them in three very straight rows of three on one sheet and two rows of three on the other. Cover with clingfilm and a tea towel and leave to rise for 1 hour.

7 About 15 minutes before the end of the rising time, preheat the oven to 220°C/425°F/gas 7/fan oven 200°C.

8 Place all the paste ingredients in a bowl and whisk vigorously with a fork until smooth. Take a plastic bag, fill it with the cross paste and direct the paste to one corner, gently twisting the top of the bag around the paste to exclude the air.

9 **NOW STOP!** *Follow all the crossing instructions carefully on page 79, steps 9–11.*

10 Bake the crossed buns for 10–13 minutes.

11 Meanwhile, prepare the glaze. Place the water and sugar in a small saucepan and stir over a low heat for about 2 minutes until the sugar dissolves. Turn up the heat, bring to the boil and simmer for 1 minute. Remove from the heat.

12 The buns are baked when they are a light golden colour and sound hollow when you tap on the base. Remove the excess cross paste and the inevitable burnt bits of fruit from the tops and transfer the buns to a wire rack.

13 While the buns are still hot, paint on the glaze with a pastry brush to make them shiny and sticky. Be careful not to press on the chocolate chunks while you are glazing or they will smear.

BREADMAKER TIPS
To make the dough, put the liquid ingredients in first, then the dry ingredients, adding the yeast last. Use the Dough programme to mix the dough and allow it to rise, then remove from the breadmaker and continue from step 4.

Lightly Spiced Wholemeal Honey Coils

These are excellent just on their own, even without butter, but you can split them and spread them with butter if you prefer. I also like them with soups. In a breadmaker, you can use the Dough programme, leaving it to rise for an extra 1 hour then continuing from step 5. See the photograph on page 2.

MAKES 14 BUNS

7 cardamom pods, split and seeds finely ground

610 g/1 lb 5½ oz wholemeal bread flour

15 g/½ oz dried milk powder (non-fat dry milk)

10 g/2 tsp salt

50 g/1¾ oz light muscovado sugar

1½ tsp ground cinnamon

⅛ tsp ground cloves

1 sachet + 1 tsp easy-blend dried yeast

1 egg, beaten

50 g/1¾ oz butter, melted

50 g/1¾ oz clear honey

280 g/10 oz warm water

1   Split the cardamom pods, remove the seeds and grind them finely using a pestle and mortar or an electric grinder.

2   Place the ground seeds and the remaining ingredients in your mixer bowl and combine with the dough hook on speed 1 for 2 minutes until you have a soft dough that doesn't smear the bottom of the bowl. You may need to add a little flour or warm water, no more than 15 g/½ oz at a time, to get the desired consistency.

3   Mix on speed 2 for 10 minutes, adding flour as needed to maintain the correct consistency. Be careful not to add too much flour and make the dough stiff and tight – leave it a little soft if you are unsure.

4   Take the dough out of the mixer, knead it a few times and mould it into a head (see page 14). Place it back in the mixing bowl, cover with clingfilm (plastic wrap) and a tea towel (dish cloth) and leave to rise for 2 hours or until doubled in size.

5   Divide the dough into fourteen 75 g/2½ oz portions and share around any leftover dough equally between them. Mould the portions round (see pages 16–17), cover and allow to rest for 10 minutes. Grease and flour two large baking (cookie) sheets or just line with non-stick liner.

6   Place the portions on your work surface. The dough has a slightly sticky texture, but it is not hard to work with and you shouldn't need extra flour for dusting. Roll one portion into a 28 cm/ 11 in sausage (see page 20).

7   Coil one end of the sausage around until you have 2.5 cm/1 in left. Tuck this in under the coil and place it on a baking sheet. Keep the shaped coils covered while you carry on with the remaining portions.

8   Cover all the coils with clingfilm and a tea towel and leave to rise for 1 hour.

9   About 15 minutes before the end of the rising time, preheat the oven to 220°C/425°F/gas 7/fan oven 200°C.

10 Bake the coils for 10–12 minutes or until golden. (I bake one sheet at a time in the centre of the oven, turning the sheet near the end of the baking time to ensure even colouring.) Transfer to a wire rack to cool.

FILLED ROLLS AND BUNS

My favourite – the funky stuff!

As a kid, a burrito was downright fascinating: all kinds of yummy stuff packed into a flour tortilla, which was folded into a cool shape so you didn't know what was in it until you took a bite. Ever since then I've loved 'wrapped-up' food – I'm also a big fan of Cornish pasties!

There's lots of cool shapes and unusual but tasty flavour combinations in this chapter. I've experimented with different ways of adding fillings to the bread dough and packed the rolls and buns full of goodies. To achieve some of the shapes, I have made use of dariol moulds, pudding basins and mini loaf tins.

Do portion the dough accurately (see page 11) to get the very best from these wonderful filled rolls and buns.

HTBs

HTB stands for Hot Tuna Bun! The buns puff up a lot while they bake and some may look as if they have lost their folded shape when they first come out of the oven. Don't worry; the tops settle down again as they cool. A 185 g/6½ oz/small can of tuna in spring water or brine will give the correct weight once drained.

MAKES 8 BUNS

FOR THE DOUGH
500 g/1 lb 2 oz strong white bread flour
5 g/1 tsp salt
5 g/1 tsp sugar
1 sachet of easy-blend dried yeast

15 g/½ oz butter, melted
300 g/10½ oz warm water

FOR THE FILLING
60 g finely chopped red onion (about 1 small onion)
40 g/1½ oz grated carrot (about 1 medium carrot)
120 g/4¼ oz tuna

¼ tsp white pepper
½ tsp salt
2 tsp dried parsley, or one heaped tablespoon chopped fresh
A pinch of cayenne or to taste
A pinch of paprika or to taste
80 g/2¾ oz crème fraîche
30 g/1 oz melted butter, for brushing

1 Place all the dough ingredients in your mixer bowl and combine with the dough hook on speed 1 for 2 minutes until you have a soft dough that doesn't smear the bottom of the bowl. You may need to add a little flour or warm water, no more than 15 g/½ oz at a time, to get the desired consistency.

2 Mix on speed 2 for 10 minutes, checking frequently to maintain the correct consistency.

3 Take the dough out of the mixer and knead it a few times. Place it back in the mixing bowl, cover with clingfilm (plastic wrap) and a tea towel (dish cloth) and leave to rise for 30 minutes or until doubled in size.

4 Meanwhile, mix together the filling ingredients. Grease and flour two baking (cookie) sheets or just line with non-stick liner.

5 Divide the dough into eight 100 g/3½ oz portions and share around any leftover dough equally between the portion. Mould the portions round (see pages 16–17), then re-cover and allow to rest for 5 minutes.

6   Roll out each ball to a 15 cm/6 in round (see pages 18–19). Keep the finished rounds covered.

7   Divide the filling between the rounds, spreading it out with the back of a spoon to cover the entire surface all the way to the edge.

8   Fold all the rounds in half, but don't seal them. Brush the tops with the melted butter.

9   Take hold of one open corner and fold it over to the other open corner. Gently press down the entire surface to maintain the shape, but without sealing them. You will now have a triangular shape with the point sealed and the widest part showing folded layers of dough and filling. Place four buns on each prepared baking sheet.

10 Brush the tops of the buns generously with melted butter, then cover lightly with clingfilm and leave to rise for about 30 minutes until puffy.

11 About 15 minutes before the end of the rising time, preheat the oven to 220°C/425°F/gas 7/ fan oven 200°C.

12 Bake the buns for 13–15 minutes or until the edges have a good golden colour but the overall bun is still quite pale.

13 Transfer the buns to a wire rack to cool. Eat hot, warm or cold. Any left over can be stored in the fridge or freezer when cold.

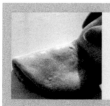

BREADMAKER TIPS
To make the dough, put the liquid ingredients in first, then the dry ingredients, adding the yeast last. Use the Dough programme to mix the dough and allow it to rise, then remove from the breadmaker and continue from step 4.

Hot New Mexico Buns

I had seen a lot of 'breakfast burritos' in New Mexico, where my parents live, and it started me thinking about chillies and Mexican cheeses, such as asadero and queso quesadilla, and about breakfast ingredients in a bun. Dad loved the results! Special thanks to Martin and Eric Campos, my official New Mexican tasters.

MAKES 8 BUNS

FOR THE DOUGH
500 g/1 lb 2 oz strong white bread flour
5 g/1 tsp salt
5 g/1 tsp caster (superfine) sugar
1 sachet of easy-blend dried yeast
15 g/½ oz butter, melted

300 g/10½ oz warm water
FOR THE FILLING
130 g/4½ oz unsmoked back bacon, roughly chopped
1 fresh green chilli, finely chopped
15 g/½ oz butter
3 eggs, lightly beaten
100 g/3½ oz crème fraîche

80 g/2¾ oz grated Caerphilly cheese
80 g/2¾ oz grated mature Cheddar cheese
2 tbsp chopped fresh chives
⅛ tsp salt
Scant ½ tsp black pepper
30 g/1 oz melted butter, for brushing

1 Place all the dough ingredients in your mixer bowl and combine with the dough hook on speed 1 for 2 minutes until you have a soft dough that doesn't smear the bottom of the bowl. You may need to add a little flour or warm water, no more than 15 g/½ oz at a time, to get the desired consistency.

2 Mix on speed 2 for 10 minutes, checking frequently to maintain the correct consistency; better a little too soft than adding too much flour.

3 Take the dough out of the mixer, knead it a few times and mould it into a head (see page 14). Place it back in the mixing bowl, cover with clingfilm (plastic wrap) and a tea towel (dish cloth) and leave to rise for 30 minutes.

4 Uncover the dough, punch it down and mould it back into a head. Re-cover and leave to rise for another 30 minutes or until it has doubled in size.

5 Meanwhile, grease and flour two baking (cookie) sheets or just line with non-stick liner. To make

the filling, fry the bacon and chilli in the butter over a medium heat for 2–3 minutes. Add the eggs and cook for 2–3 minutes until scrambled but not overly dry. Transfer to a plate and allow to cool.

6   Mix together the crème fraîche, cheeses, chives, salt and pepper in a bowl.

7   Divide the dough into eight 100 g/3½ oz portions and share around any leftover dough equally between the portions. Mould the portions round (see pages 16–17), then cover and allow to rest for 5 minutes.

8   Roll out each ball to a 15 cm/6 in round (see pages 18–19). Keep the finished rounds covered.

9   Add the cooled egg mixture to the cheese mixture and stir thoroughly.

10 Divide the filling between the rounds, spreading it out with the back of a spoon to cover the entire surface all the way to the edge. Fold all the rounds in half, but don't seal them. Brush the tops with the melted butter.

11 Take hold of one open corner and fold it over to the other open corner. Gently press down the entire surface to maintain the shape, but without sealing them. You will now have a triangular shape with the point sealed and the widest part showing folded layers of dough and filling. Place four buns on each prepared baking sheet.

12 Brush the tops of the buns generously with melted butter, then cover lightly with clingfilm and leave to rise for 30 minutes.

13 About 15 minutes before the end of the rising time, preheat the oven to 220°C/425°F/gas 7/fan oven 200°C.

14 Bake the buns for 13–15 minutes or until the edges have a good golden colour but the overall bun is still quite pale.

15 Transfer the buns to a wire rack to cool. Eat hot, warm or cold. Any left over can be stored in the fridge or freezer when cold (they freeze and reheat very well).

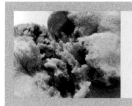

BREADMAKER TIPS
To make the dough, put the liquid ingredients in first, then the dry ingredients, adding the yeast last. Use the Dough programme to mix the dough and allow it to rise, then remove from the breadmaker and continue from step 5.

Rumpled Pizza

These look very smart served with a salad, and they taste great, especially the nice crusty bits! You can vary the filling as you like – fancy mushrooms, cheeses, fresh herbs or a dollop of crème fraîche in each one is gorgeous. I recommend two per person for a main meal. They work just as well made in ramekins (custard cups).

MAKES 8 BUNS

FOR THE DOUGH

450 g/15½ oz strong white bread flour

5 g/1 tsp caster (superfine) sugar

5 g/1 tsp salt

1 sachet of easy-blend dried yeast

20 g/¾ oz sun-dried tomato oil, from the jar

250 g/9 oz warm water

FOR THE FILLING

115 g/4 oz mixed sweet (bell) peppers, chopped

50 g/1¾ oz onion, finely chopped

85 g/3 oz mushrooms, chopped

50 g/1¾ oz stoned (pitted) black olives, sliced

100 g/3½ oz sun-dried tomatoes, chopped

20 g/¾ oz sun-dried tomato oil, from the jar

1 heaped tsp dried oregano

¼ tsp garlic powder

¼ tsp salt

¼ tsp white or black pepper

200 g/7 oz grated Mozzarella or mature Cheddar cheese

30 g/1 oz sun-dried tomato oil from the jar, for brushing

1   Place all the dough ingredients in your mixer bowl and combine with the dough hook on speed 1 for 2 minutes until you have a soft dough that doesn't smear the bottom of the mixing bowl. You may need to add a little flour or warm water, no more than 15 g/½ oz at a time, to get the desired consistency.

2   Mix on speed 2 for 10 minutes, making sure the dough stays at the right consistency. Add a bit more flour if you need to.

3   Take the dough out of the mixer, knead it a few times and mould it into a head (see page 14). The dough has a slightly sticky texture, so you may need just a light dusting of flour. Place it back in the mixing bowl, cover with clingfilm (plastic wrap) and a tea towel (dish cloth) and leave to rise for 30 minutes.

4   Meanwhile, mix together all the filling ingredients except the cheese in a bowl. Cover and set aside to allow the flavours to combine and the mushrooms to marinate.

5 Uncover the dough, punch it down and mould it back into a head. Re-cover and leave to rise for another 30 minutes or until it has doubled in size.

6 Divide the dough into eight 90 g/3 oz portions and share around any leftover dough equally between the portions. Mould round (see pages 16–17), cover and allow to rest for 5 minutes. This resting makes the dough easier to roll out. Meanwhile grease and flour eight mini loaf tins (pans) and place them all on a baking (cooking) sheet.

7 Using some flour for dusting, roll out each ball to a 15 cm/6 in round (see pages 18–19). Keep the finished rounds covered while you roll out the rest.

8 Place the sun-dried tomato oil for brushing in a small bowl or ramekin (custard cup).

9 Lay out all the rounds. Mix the cheese into the filling and place an equal amount on each round, keeping it fairly central. Fold all the rounds in half, but don't seal them. Brush the tops with the sun-dried tomato oil.

10 Carefully, pick up one of the folded rounds and brush the other side with the oil. Then, keeping all the edges of that folded round to the top, gently place it in a mini loaf tin. You want them to gape open and have rumpled edges – the more folds and bits of filling showing, the better the finished rumpled pizza will look. Repeat with the remaining rounds.

11 Cover the pizzas with clingfilm and allow to rest for 20–30 minutes until puffy. Preheat the oven to 200°C/400°F/gas 6/fan oven 180°C.

12 Bake for 20–22 minutes until golden. Leave them in their tins for a minute or two, then transfer to a wire rack to cool a little before eating. Any left over can be stored in the fridge or freezer.

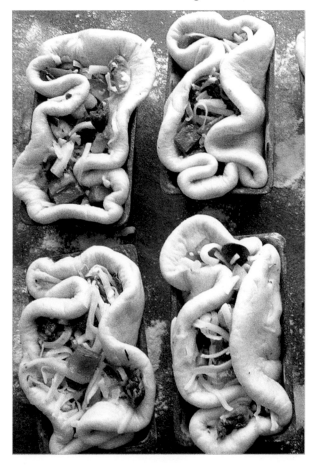

BREADMAKER TIPS
To make the dough, put the liquid ingredients in first, then the dry ingredients, adding the yeast last. Use the Dough programme to mix the dough and allow it to rise, then continue from step 6, but have the filling mixed as at step 4 before removing the dough from the machine.

Apple and Anise Crinkle Buns

I first tried apple and anise together in New Mexico when I was visiting my parents, and I was very impressed with how well the flavours work together. Naturally, I had to have a go at combining the flavours in my own recipes and here's the result of my experimenting for you to enjoy – delicious!

MAKES 6 BUNS

FOR THE DOUGH
280 g/10 oz strong white bread flour
$\frac{1}{2}$ tsp salt
$\frac{1}{2}$ tsp whole anise seeds
30 g/1 oz light muscovado sugar

1 sachet of easy-blend dried yeast
30 g/1 oz butter, melted
150 g/5 oz warm water
FOR THE FILLING
360 g/12¾ oz peeled and thinly sliced eating (dessert) apple (about 3 large apples)
70 g/2½ oz light muscovado sugar

20 g/¾ oz plain (all-purpose) flour
$\frac{1}{2}$ tsp ground cinnamon
30 g/1 oz butter, for brushing
FOR THE TOPPING
60 g/2 oz icing (confectioners') sugar, sifted
A little hot water

1   Place all the dough ingredients in your mixer bowl and combine with the dough hook on speed 1 for 2 minutes until you have a soft dough that doesn't smear the bottom of the bowl. You may need to add a little flour or warm water, no more than 15 g/½ oz at a time, to get the desired consistency.

2   Mix on speed 2 for 10 minutes, making sure the dough stays at the right consistency.

3   Take the dough out of the mixer, knead it a few times and mould it into a head (see page 14). Place it back in the mixing bowl, cover with clingfilm (plastic wrap) and a tea towel (dish cloth) and leave to rise for 1 hour or until doubled in size.

4   Grease and flour six 10 cm/4 in tart tins (patty pans) and place them on a baking (cookie) sheet.

5   Divide the dough into six 80 g/2¾ oz portions and share around any leftover dough equally between the portions. Mould round (see pages 16–17), cover and allow to rest for 10 minutes.

6   Meanwhile, peel the apples and finely slice them by hand or with a food processor. Tip them into a large bowl, add the remaining filling ingredients and mix together thoroughly.

7   Using flour for dusting, roll each portion of dough to a 13 cm/5 in round (see pages 18–19).

8   Brush all the rounds with butter. Pick up one round and brush the other side with butter, then ease it into the prepared tart tin. There is no need to press the dough into the tin's crinkles as the bread will expand into them as it rises. Repeat with the remaining rounds.

9   Place one lined tart tin on your scale, get a zero setting and fill the tart with 70 g/2½ oz of the apple filling. Repeat with the others.

10 Cover the buns with clingfilm and a tea towel and allow to rise for 20 minutes. Preheat the oven to 200°C/400°F/gas 6/fan oven 180°C.

11 Bake the buns for 12–16 minutes. You may need to turn the sheet near the end of the baking time to ensure even colouring.

12 Mix the icing sugar with the water until smooth – start with only about ½ tbsp of water but you may need a little more. There are several ways to get the drizzle effect on top of the buns. You can add a tiny bit more water to make the icing (frosting) thin enough to run off the tip of a spoon. Or you can make a piping bag from greaseproof paper, or from a plastic bag with a tiny corner snipped off. No matter which way you choose to apply the topping, remember that you are not drawing lines across the bun – you are drizzling.

13 Carefully lift the crinkle buns out of the tins and place them on wire cooling rack. The drizzling can be done while they are still warm or after they have cooled. If you are using a spoon, start in front of the bun, let the icing start to drizzle off the spoon, then flick your wrist back and forth. Continue this motion at an even speed over the bun and beyond it. If you are using a piping bag, use the same wrist motion while applying even pressure to the bag.

BREADMAKER TIPS
To make the dough, put the liquid ingredients in first, then the dry ingredients, adding the yeast last. Use the Dough programme to mix the dough and allow it to rise, then remove from the breadmaker and continue from step 4.

Corin's Oaty Strawberry Pots

This is the result of my son Corin's request for strawberry bread – best eaten sliced in half lengthways, he assures me! Make sure the strawberries are at room temperature; you wouldn't want to add cold strawberries to warm dough. You could try combinations of other soft fruits for a change, which might look very pretty.

MAKES 12 BUNS

FOR THE DOUGH
35 g/1¼ oz toasted porridge oats
200 g/7 oz water just off the boil
30 g/1 oz butter, melted

310 g/11 oz strong white bread flour
5 g/1 tsp salt
30 g/1 oz dark muscovado sugar or
   molasses sugar
1 sachet of easy-blend dried yeast

FOR THE FILLING
70 g/2½ oz vanilla sugar
¾ tsp cornflour (cornstarch)
330 g/11½ oz strawberries, cut into large
   chunks

1 Preheat the oven to 180°C/350°F/gas 4/fan oven 160°C. Place the oats on a baking (cookie) sheet and toast them in the oven for 14 minutes. They will only colour slightly but the toasting makes all the difference to their flavour. Turn the oven off.

2 Put the toasted oats in your mixing bowl and stir in the water. Leave to cool for 30 minutes, stirring from time to time.

3 Meanwhile, grease 12 dariol moulds with the melted butter. I find the easiest way to do this is to paint it on to the moulds with a pastry brush. Dust lightly with flour.

4 Place the oats and water in your mixing bowl and add all the remaining dough ingredients. Combine with the dough hook on speed 1 for 2 minutes. You will need to stop the mixer and push the flour down to make a smooth dough that doesn't smear the bottom of the bowl. Add 15 g/½ oz of warm water (this will initially make the dough very soft, but it will absorb the extra water during the next mix).

5 Mix on speed 2 for 10 minutes, making sure the dough stays at the right consistency.

6   Take the dough out of the mixer, knead it a few times and mould it into a head (see page 14). Place it back in the mixing bowl, cover with clingfilm (plastic wrap) and a tea towel (dish cloth) and leave to rise for 1 hour (it doesn't rise a great deal).

7   Punch the dough down and divide it into twelve 45 g/1½ oz portions. Mould them round (see pages 16–17), cover and allow the portions to rest for 5 minutes.

8   Roll out each portion to a 15 cm/6 in round (see pages 18–19), using a little bread flour for dusting.

9   Gather up a round of dough and ease it to the bottom of a prepared dariol mould. Press the dough very firmly against the sides of the mould using your fingers without making any holes (if you do just press more dough over the hole). You may need to dust your fingers with a little flour. Don't worry about different dough thicknesses inside the dariol mould, or about bits sticking out of the top – they make it easy to lift the finished bread out of the mould. Repeat with all the dough rounds, keeping the finished moulds covered as you line the rest.

10 Add the vanilla sugar and cornflour to the strawberries and stir thoroughly. Place equal amounts of the strawberry filling in each lined mould, sharing any juices around. The amount of filling may seem a bit mean at this stage but it won't be when the breads are finished. Place the dariol moulds on a baking (cookie) sheet and leave to rise for 20–30 minutes.

11 About 15 minutes before the end of the rising time, preheat the oven to 180°C/350°F/gas 4/fan oven 160°C.

12 Bake the strawberry pots on the central oven shelf for 15–17 minutes until the tops are just turning golden brown.

13 Remove from the oven and let the moulds rest on the baking sheet for 5 minutes, then lift the breads out of their moulds using the sticking-out bits (you may also need to loosen the edges with a butter knife) and place on a wire rack.

14 Let the breads cool quite a bit before eating. It's no fun shifting hot strawberries around in your mouth as you try not to burn your tongue if you're over-eager to try them. I speak from experience!

BREADMAKER TIPS
To make the dough, put the liquid ingredients in first, then the dry ingredients, adding the yeast last. Use the Dough programme to mix the dough and allow it to rise, then continue from step 7, having prepared the dariol moulds as in step 3 before removing the dough from the machine.

Liquorice Buns

I love the way these look. It isn't difficult to colour the coconut as long as you make sure you give it time – possibly days – to dry so you don't lose any colour when you mix it into the dough. If you can't find liquorice root (and it can be difficult), you can use ground aniseed instead. They are both very tasty.

MAKES 9 BUNS

FOR THE FILLING
30 g/1 oz sweetened desiccated (shredded) coconut
1/8 tsp each pink, yellow and blue food colouring

FOR THE DOUGH
400 g/14 oz strong white bread flour
5 g/1 tsp salt
50 g/1¾ oz caster (superfine) sugar
2 tbsp finely ground liquorice root
1 sachet of easy-blend dried yeast
20 g/¾ oz butter, melted
1 egg, beaten
185 g/6½ oz warm water

FOR THE EGG WASH
1 egg yolk mixed with 15 g/½ oz water
TO FINISH
240 g/8½ oz icing (confectioners') sugar, sifted
30 g/2 tbsp hot water
9 liquorice candies

1   The night, or a few days, before making the buns, divide the coconut between three small bowls or ramekins (custard cups). Mix one with each food colour, allow to dry completely and then cover until needed.

2   Place all the dough ingredients in your mixer bowl and combine with the dough hook on speed 1 for 2 minutes until you have a soft dough that doesn't smear the bottom of the bowl. You may need to add a little flour or warm water, no more than 15 g/½ oz at a time, to get the desired consistency.

3   Mix on speed 2 for 10 minutes. Keep an eye on the consistency throughout; better a bit too soft than adding to much flour.

4   Take the dough out of the mixer, knead it a few times and mould it into a head (see page 14). Place it back in the mixing bowl, cover with clingfilm (plastic wrap) and a tea towel (dish cloth) and leave to rise for 1½ hours (it doesn't rise a great deal).

5   Grease and flour a baking (cookie) sheet or just line with non-stick liner. Mix the three coconut colours together.

6   Knock the dough back, take it out of the mixing bowl and flatten it out a bit on your work surface.

7   Put the coloured coconut on the middle of the dough and wrap the edges round to enclose it. Using your scraper, chop the coconut into the dough until it is evenly distributed (see page 23).

8   Divide the dough into nine 80 g/2³⁄₄ oz portions and share around any leftover dough equally between the portions. Mould round (see pages 16–17) and place on the baking sheet.

9   Cover with clingfilm and a tea towel and leave to rise for 45 minutes. Again, they won't rise a great deal, but they do spring in the oven.

10 About 15 minutes before the end of the rising time, preheat the oven to 220°C/425°F/gas 7/fan oven 200°C.

11 Brush the buns with the egg wash and bake for 10–12 minutes or until golden. Check about 3 minutes before the end of the cooking time to see if you need to turn the sheet so all the buns colour evenly.

12 Transfer to a wire rack to cool completely (though you can eat them warm from the oven if you decide to omit the decoration).

13 Sift the icing sugar into a bowl. Add the hot water and stir until smooth. You may need to add just a little more water.

14 Hold a roll around the middle with your fingers down towards the bottom. Dip the cold rolls into the icing (frosting), stopping before you reach your fingers and letting the excess icing drain back into the bowl before turning the bun right side up again. Be patient!

15 Repeat with the remaining buns, placing them back on the cooling rack as they are dipped. Let the icing dry a little, then place a liquorice candy on top of each bun.

BREADMAKER TIPS
To make the dough, put the liquid ingredients in first, then the dry ingredients, adding the yeast last. Use the Dough programme to mix the dough and allow it to rise. Leave it in the breadmaker for an extra 30 minutes to continue to rise, then remove from the breadmaker and continue from step 5. Colour the coconut beforehand as at step 1.

Sunflower Honey Buns

These have a nice chewy sweetness about them and are very easy to make – I promise! You don't have to colour the dough if you don't want to; I just thought it would be fun. I like to warm one of these through in the oven for breakfast because they look so inviting and cheery next to a big mug of tea.

MAKES 4 BUNS

FOR THE DOUGH
265 g/9½ oz strong white bread flour
5 g/1 tsp salt
5 g/1 tsp caster (superfine) sugar

5 g/1 tsp easy-blend dried yeast
10 g/2 tsp honey
10 g/2 tsp oil
5 g/1 tsp yellow food colouring
135 g/4¼ oz warm water

FOR THE FILLING
20 g/¾ oz honey

FOR THE TOPPING
25 g/1 oz clear honey
40 g/1½ oz sunflower seeds

1 Place all the dough ingredients in your mixer bowl and combine with the dough hook on speed 1 for 2 minutes until you have a soft dough that doesn't smear the bottom of the bowl. You may need to add a little flour or warm water, no more than 15 g/½ oz at a time, to get the desired consistency.

2 Mix on speed 2 for 10 minutes.

3 Take the dough out of the mixer, knead it a few times and mould it into a head (see page 14). Place it back in the mixing bowl, cover with clingfilm (plastic wrap) and a tea towel (dish cloth) and leave to rise for 30 minutes.

4 Knock back the dough, mould it back into a head, re-cover and leave to rise for a further 30 minutes or until doubled in size.

5 Divide the dough into four 40 g/1½ oz portions and four 65 g/2¼ oz portions. Mould all the portions round (see pages 16–17), cover and allow to rest while you prepare the patty tin (pan) and the topping ingredients.

6 Grease and flour the patty tin (this will help if any honey runs underneath the buns, which

could make them stick to the tin). Place the honey for the topping in a microwavable ramekin (custard cup) or in a small saucepan. Place the sunflower seeds on a small plate.

7   Roll out all the smaller portions to 6 cm/2½ in rounds (see pages 18–19). Cover and set aside. Roll out all the larger portions to 15 cm/6 in rounds.

8   Using your metal scraper, starting from the outside edge of one of the larger rounds, make a 4 cm/1½ in cut towards the centre. Continue round, leaving about 2.5 cm/1 in between cuts at the outside edge – the cuts will be closer together as they approach the middle, which will be solid.

9   Slide the scraper under the cut round and use it to carry the round to the patty tin. Place it in one of the sections.

10 With your left hand, take hold of one of the 2.5 cm/1 in wide dough edges. Put your right index finger under the middle of the piece of dough and rest it there. Wrap the dough lightly around your finger using the thumb and forefinger of your left hand. Keep your left hand on the dough, remove your right finger and then pinch the ends together with your left hand. Do this all the way around the round and you will have flower petals! Repeat these steps with the other three rounds. You can reverse the left and right instructions if you find this easier, as long as you stick to it.

11 Using a teaspoon, place a quarter of the honey for the filling in the solid centre of each round.

12 Warm the honey for the topping to make it easier to brush the dough – but don't make it scalding hot. Take one of the smaller rounds, brush the top and sides with the honey and then gently press it into the sunflower seeds on the plate. Be sure to get seeds on the sides as well.

13 Place the seed-covered round in the middle of one of the flower shapes. Repeat with the remaining smaller rounds. Cover the buns with clingfilm and allow to rise for 30 minutes.

14 Bake in a preheated oven at 180°C/350°F/ gas 4/fan oven 160°C for 15–18 minutes. Allow to rest in the patty tin for a couple of minutes, then transfer to a wire rack to cool.

BREADMAKER TIPS
To make the dough, put the liquid ingredients in first, then the dry ingredients, adding the yeast last. Use the Dough programme to mix the dough and allow it to rise, then remove from the breadmaker and continue from step 5.

Marzipan Bars

These always taste Christmassy to me, as I associate marzipan with the festive season. The bars of marzipan are placed inside the individual loaves so the dough bakes around them – absolutely delicious. Change the shape if you don't have mini loaf tins; ramekins (custard cups) or pudding basins will work.

MAKES 8 INDIVIDUAL LOAVES

FOR THE DOUGH
515 g/1 lb 2½ oz strong white bread flour
5 g/1 tsp salt
50 g/1¾ oz caster (superfine) sugar

1 sachet of easy-blend dried yeast
15 g/½ oz butter, melted
5 g/1 tsp almond essence (extract)
Zest of 1 lemon
1 egg, beaten
250 g/9 oz warm water

FOR THE FILLING
185 g/6½ oz marzipan
30 g/1 oz mixed (candied) peel
15 g/½ oz amaretto liqueur

1   Place all the dough ingredients in your mixer bowl and combine with the dough hook on speed 1 for 2 minutes until you have a soft dough that doesn't smear the bottom of the bowl. You may need to add a little flour or warm water, no more than 15 g/½ oz at a time, to get the desired consistency.

2   Mix on speed 2 for 10 minutes and check frequently to maintain a soft dough that isn't smearing the bottom.

3   Take the dough out of the mixer, knead it a few times and mould it into a head (see page 14). Place it back in the mixing bowl, cover with clingfilm (plastic wrap) and a tea towel (dish cloth) and leave to rise for 1 hour. The dough has a sticky texture, so you may need a light dusting of bread flour.

4   Meanwhile, combine the filling ingredients by kneading them together with your fingers. Divide the mixture into eight equal portions and roll out each to a 9 cm/3½ in sausage or 'bar'. You can do this between your hands but it is quite sticky so you may need to dust them with a little icing sugar. Dust the portions with icing sugar and

store them in an airtight container until you are ready to use them.

5   Divide the dough into eight 105 g/3½ oz portions and share around any leftover dough equally between the portions. Mould the portions round (see pages 16–17), then cover and leave to rest for 5 minutes.

6   Meanwhile, grease and flour eight mini loaf tins. Place them all on a solid baking (cookie) sheet.

7   Using bread flour for dusting, roll out each portion to a 15 cm/6 in round (see pages 18–19). Keep the finished rounds covered while you work on the others.

8   Lay out all the rounds and place a marzipan 'bar' horizontally close to the top of each round.

9   Take the top edge of one of the rounds and fold it over the marzipan. Then continue rolling and stop when the seam is on the bottom.

10 Pick up the roll, fold both ends in towards the bottom and place it in a prepared tin. Repeat with the remaining rounds.

11 Give the loaves a very light dusting of flour, then cover lightly with clingfilm and a tea towel and leave to rise for 30 minutes.

12 About 15 minutes before the end of the rising time, preheat the oven to 220°C/425°F/gas 7/fan oven 200°C.

13 Bake for 12–15 minutes or until the loaves are a light golden colour.

14 Transfer to a wire rack to cool.

BREADMAKER TIPS
To make the dough, put the liquid ingredients in first, then the dry ingredients, adding the yeast last. Use the Dough programme to mix the dough and allow it to rise, then remove from the breadmaker and continue from step 4.

Cinnamon, Chocolate and Marshmallow Dunking Buns

I love eating these. I have so much fun prising off the wonky cinnamon-encrusted top, then tearing up the bun and dunking it into the molten chocolate and marshmallows. I end up with chocolate and spice all over my fingers and down my chin – aaahhh! I should add that I usually eat them when I'm alone!

MAKES 8 BUNS

FOR THE DOUGH
300 g/10½ oz strong white bread flour
½ tsp salt
1 sachet of easy-blend dried yeast

10 g/2 tsp dried milk powder (non-fat dry milk)
1 heaped tsp ground cinnamon
25 g/1 oz light muscovado sugar
15 g/½ oz butter, melted
170 g/6 oz warm water

FOR THE FILLING
150 g/5 oz plain (semi-sweet) chocolate, chopped into small chunks
50 g/1¾ oz mini marshmallows
10 g/2 tsp Cinnamon Sugar Mix (see opposite), for sprinkling
30 g/1 oz melted butter, for brushing

1   Place all the dough ingredients in your mixer bowl and combine with the dough hook on speed 1 for 2 minutes until you have a soft dough that doesn't smear the bottom of the bowl. You may need to add a little flour or warm water, no more than 15 g/½ oz at a time, to get the desired consistency.

2   Mix on speed 2 for 10 minutes, adding flour or water as needed to maintain the correct consistency.

3   Take the dough out of the mixer, knead it a few times and mould it into a head (see page 14). Place it back in the mixing bowl, cover with clingfilm (plastic wrap) and a tea towel (dish cloth) and leave to rise for 1 hour.

4   Grease and flour eight individual pudding basins and place them all on a baking (cookie) sheet.

5   Divide the dough into eight 65 g/2 oz portions and share around any leftover dough equally between the portions. Mould them round (see pages 16–17). Cover and leave to rest while you prepare the filling.

6 Combine the filling ingredients in a small bowl. Stir thoroughly (you will also need to keep stirring as you use the filling to keep the sugar mixed in with the marshmallows and chocolate).

7 Using bread flour for dusting, roll out each portion into a 15 cm/6 in round (see pages 18–19). Share the filling equally between the rounds, piling it into the centre.

8 Dampen the edges of the rounds with a little water. Fold all the rounds in half and seal the edges completely by pressing them firmly together.

9 Brush all over the top surface with melted butter. Carefully pick up each parcel and brush the other side with melted butter. Then gently squash the two narrow ends in towards the middle like an accordion or closing a paper fan. The top of the bun will form a wonky ridge.

10 Place each parcel in a pudding basin and sprinkle generously with the cinnamon sugar mix.

11 Cover with clingfilm and a tea towel and allow the parcels to rest for 20 minutes. Preheat the oven to 220°C/425°F/gas 7/fan oven 200°C.

12 Bake the parcels for 10–12 minutes. Lift them out of their basins and check to make sure they sound hollow when you tap the base.

13 Transfer to a wire rack and allow to cool for 5 minutes.

14 To serve, watching out for steam, tear or slice the top off of the bun. Tear off pieces of the lid and

dunk them into the filling. Then gobble the rest of the bun.

15 To reheat, pop the buns in the oven at 180°C/ 350°F/gas 4/fan oven 160°C for 6–7 minutes.

CINNAMON SUGAR MIX

5 g/1 tsp ground cinnamon

80 g/2³/₄ oz granulated sugar

Mix together and use as required. This quantity is more than enough for this recipe. The remainder can be stored in an airtight container.

BREADMAKER TIPS

To make the dough, put the liquid ingredients in first, then the dry ingredients, adding the yeast last. Use the Dough programme to mix the dough and allow it to rise, then remove from the breadmaker and continue from step 4.

Chocolate, Coconut and Marshmallow Dunking Buns

I love the look of the coconut encrusted around the bun when I make these delicious dunking buns! To eat them, you tear off the top, then dip it into the melted centre. Very messy, of course, but absolutely delicious and the perfect treat for children (and for those who are still children at heart!).

MAKES 8 BUNS

FOR THE DOUGH
265 g/9½ oz strong white bread flour
35 g/1¼ oz cocoa (unsweetened chocolate) powder
5 g/½ tsp salt

10 g/2 tsp dried milk powder (non-fat dry milk)
25 g/1 oz dark muscovado sugar
1 sachet of easy-blend dried yeast
15 g/½ oz butter, melted
170 g/6 oz warm water

FOR THE FILLING
150 g/5 oz white chocolate with coconut, chopped into small chunks
60 g/2 oz mini marshmallows
30 g/1 oz melted butter, for brushing
50 g/1¾ oz sweetened desiccated (shredded) coconut, for sprinkling

1. Place all the dough ingredients in your mixer bowl and combine with the dough hook on speed 1 for 2 minutes until you have a soft dough that doesn't smear the bottom of the bowl. You may need to add a little flour or warm water, no more than 15 g/½ oz at a time, to get the desired consistency.

2. Mix on speed 2 for 10 minutes, adding flour or water as needed to maintain the correct consistency.

3. Take the dough out of the mixer, knead it a few times and mould it into a head (see page 14). Place it back in the mixing bowl, cover with clingfilm (plastic wrap) and a tea towel (dish cloth) and leave to rise for 1 hour.

4. Grease and flour eight individual pudding basins and place them all on a baking (cookie) sheet.

5. Divide the dough into eight equal 65 g/2 oz portions and share around any leftover dough equally between the portions. Mould them round (see pages 16–17). Cover and leave to rest while you prepare the filling.

6 Combine the chocolate and marshmallows in a small bowl.

7 Using bread flour for dusting, roll out each portion into a 15 cm/6 in round (see pages 18–19). Share the filling equally between the rounds, piling it into the centre.

8 Dampen the edges of the rounds slightly with a little water. You can use your finger or a pastry brush for this. Fold all the rounds in half and seal the edges completely by pressing them firmly together.

9 Brush all over the top surface with melted butter. Carefully pick up each parcel and brush the other side with melted butter. Then gently squash the two narrow ends in towards the middle like an accordion or closing a paper fan. The top of the bun will form a wonky ridge.

10 Place each parcel in a pudding basin and return the basins to the baking sheet. Generously sprinkle each with the sweetened desiccated coconut. Allow the parcels to rest, covered with clingfilm and a tea towel, for 20 minutes.

11 Preheat the oven to 220°C/425°F/gas 7/fan oven 200°C.

12 Bake the parcels for 10–12 minutes. Lift them out of their basins and check to make sure they sound hollow when you tap the base.

13 Transfer to a wire rack and allow to cool for 5 minutes.

14 To serve, watching out for steam, tear or slice the top off of the bun. Tear off pieces of the lid and dunk them into the filling. Then gobble the rest of the bun.

15 To reheat, pop the buns in the oven at 180°C/ 350°F/gas 4/fan oven 160°C for 7–8 minutes.

BREADMAKER TIPS

To make the dough, put the liquid ingredients in first, then the dry ingredients, adding the yeast last. Use the Dough programme to mix the dough and allow it to rise, then remove from the breadmaker and continue from step 4.

Condensed Milk Dunking Buns

These are dedicated to Claire, my Cake Dec instructor, who suggested I make a bread with condensed milk. This is one of the rare occasions that I suggest letting the bread cool for half an hour before you eat it so that the condensed milk comes back to its true character; if you can't wait for it to cool, it will still be thin.

MAKES 8 BUNS

FOR THE DOUGH
300 g/10½ oz strong white bread flour
½ tsp salt
10 g/2 tsp dried milk powder (non-fat dry milk)

7.5 g/1½ tsp ground cinnamon
30 g/1 oz light muscovado sugar
1 sachet of easy-blend dried yeast
15 g/½ oz butter, melted
170 g/6 oz warm water

FOR THE FILLING
1 x 397 g/13 oz/large can of condensed milk
30 g/1 oz melted butter, for brushing
Cinnamon Sugar Mix (see page 101), for sprinkling

1 Place all the dough ingredients in your mixer bowl and combine with the dough hook on speed 1 for 2 minutes until you have a soft dough that doesn't smear the bottom of the bowl. You may need to add a little flour or warm water, no more than 15 g/½ oz at a time, to get the desired consistency.

2 Mix on speed 2 for 10 minutes, adding flour or water as needed to maintain the correct consistency.

3 Take the dough out of the mixer, knead it a few times and mould it into a head (see page 14). Place it back in the mixing bowl, cover with clingfilm (plastic wrap) and a tea towel (dish cloth) and leave to rise for 1 hour.

4 Grease and flour eight individual pudding basins and place them all on a baking (cookie) sheet.

5 Divide the dough into eight equal 65 g/2 oz portions and share around any leftover dough equally between the portions. Mould them round (see pages 16–17). Cover and leave to rest for 5 minutes.

6   Using bread flour for dusting, roll out each portion into a 15 cm/6 in round (see pages 18–19). Brush the top surface of each with melted butter.

7   Carefully pick up a round and gently lay it, butter-side down, on top of one of the prepared pudding basins, allowing the dough to dip into the basin slightly. Spoon, or pour from a small jug, 45 g/1²/₃ oz of the condensed milk into the middle of the dough (I place the basin and the dough on my scale, set the scale to zero and then weigh in the condensed milk). Carefully gather up all the edges, pinch together and gently twist the edges shut like a sweet (candy) wrapper. Ease the parcel into the basin and return it to the baking sheet. Repeat with the remaining rounds.

8   Brush any remaining melted butter on the topknots of the parcels and sprinkle each parcel with ¹/₂ tsp of the cinnamon sugar mix. Cover the parcels with clingfilm and a tea towel and leave to rest for 30 minutes.

9   About 15 minutes before the end of the resting time, preheat the oven to 220°C/425°F/gas 7/fan oven 200°C.

10 Bake the parcels for 10–13 minutes.

11 The cinnamon sugar tends to stick so, to remove the parcels from the basins, I would suggest holding the basin in a tea towel in one hand and loosening round the edges with a butter knife. Then take the basin close to the cooling rack and lift the parcel out of its tin and on to the rack in as small a movement as possible. You don't want to tear the buns open just yet!

12 Allow the buns to cool for 30 minutes.

13 To serve, carefully tear or slice the top off of the bun (you need to go a bit further down for these than for the other dunking buns). If necessary, lift a few bits of dough out of your well of condensed milk to get a bigger opening for dunking. Tear off pieces of the lid and dunk them into the condensed milk.

14 Any buns left over can be stored after cooling in an airtight container in the fridge. To reheat, pop them in the oven at 180°C/350°F/gas 4/fan oven 160°C for 7–8 minutes.

BREADMAKER TIPS

To make the dough, put the liquid ingredients in first, then the dry ingredients, adding the yeast last. Use the Dough programme to mix the dough and allow it to rise, then remove from the breadmaker and continue from step 4.

Toasted Golden Oat Swirls

I came up with this recipe after eating porridge with golden syrup one morning, which I consider a most delicious breakfast, by the way. I thought, if it's this good in a bowl, think how wonderful oats and golden syrup would taste in a bun! Now you can find out. The lovely topping really is 'the icing on the cake'!

MAKES 15 BUNS

FOR THE DOUGH
565 g/1 lb 4 oz strong white bread flour
200 g/7 oz porridge oats
10 g/2 tsp salt
30 g/1 oz caster (superfine) sugar
2 sachets + 1 tsp easy-blend dried yeast

50 g/1³/₄ oz golden (light corn) syrup
100 g/3¹/₂ oz butter, melted
1 egg, beaten
310 g/11 oz warm water
FOR THE FILLING
100 g/3¹/₂ oz jumbo oats
100 g/3¹/₂ oz butter, very soft
100 g/3¹/₂ oz golden syrup

20 g/³/₄ oz vegetable or sunflower oil, for brushing
FOR THE TOPPING
370 g/13 oz icing (confectioners') sugar, sifted
45 g/1²/₃ oz golden syrup
45 g/1²/₃ oz hot water

1 Place all the dough ingredients in your mixer bowl and combine with the dough hook on speed 1 for 2 minutes until you have a soft dough, then add 15 g/¹/₂ oz of warm water. The dough will be a bit too soft but the oats will absorb the extra water as the dough continues to mix.

2 Mix on speed 2 for 5 minutes. Add another 15 g/¹/₂ oz of warm water. The dough will go all silly but don't panic; the extra water will be absorbed. Continue to mix on speed 2 for a further 5 minutes.

3 Take the dough out of the mixer, knead it a few times and mould it into a head (see page 14). Place it back in the mixing bowl, cover with clingfilm (plastic wrap) and a tea towel (dish cloth) and leave to rise for 1¹/₂ hours.

4 Meanwhile, toast the jumbo oats in a preheated oven at 180°C/350°F/gas 4/fan oven 160°C for 14 minutes. Set aside to cool. Turn the oven off.

5 Knock the dough back, knead it a few times and reshape it into a head. Re-cover and leave to rest for 10 minutes.

6 Grease and flour a 33 x 23 cm/13 x 9 in baking tin (pan). Combine the cooled oats and the remaining filling ingredients in a small bowl.

7 Roll the head of dough into a fat sausage (see page 20), then gently mush the dough down evenly so you can begin rolling it into a rectangle. Roll out the dough into a 68 x 43 cm/ 27 x 17 in rectangle (see pages 21–22). Gently spread the filling evenly all over the dough, but leaving a 2.5 cm/1 in uncovered border along the bottom of the longer edge. It takes time to spread the filling evenly and the amount will look rather sparse, but all will be well! Dampen the uncovered border with water using your fingertips (this is to seal the dough together when you finish rolling it up).

8 Starting at the top of the long covered edge, begin to curl the edge over on to the dough, working towards you. Try to make this first curl small and close as this will be the centre of your buns. Then carefully and slowly roll the dough towards you, trying to keep the forming sausage the same thickness. If the ends are becoming too short, you can gently stretch them to fit.

9 You are aiming to get a 76 cm/30 in long sausage so, starting with your hands in the middle, gently roll the sausage and work your hands slowly from the middle towards the outside edges as you roll. If the ends of the sausage are really ragged or very thin, just trim these off a little with a knife.

10 When it is the right length, brush the entire sausage with the oil (this will enable you to separate the rolls after they are baked).

11 Using a ruler, mark off three 25 cm/10 in sections by pressing gently with a knife. Then, within each of these sections, mark at 5 cm/2 in intervals so you end up with five sections from each 25 cm/10 in section, or 15 sections in all. Using a sawing (not cutting) action with a large serrated knife, cut through each of the marks. Place the buns spiral-side up in the prepared pan in five rows of three buns each.

12 Cover the pan with clingfilm and a tea towel and allow the buns to rise for 45 minutes.

13 About 15 minutes before the end of the rising time, preheat the oven to 180°C/350°F/gas 4/fan oven 160°C.

14 Bake on the middle oven shelf for 30–33 minutes until lightly golden.

15 Remove the buns from the oven and allow to cool in the pan while you mix up the topping. Sift the icing sugar into a large bowl. Add the syrup and hot water and mix thoroughly with a spoon until smooth.

16 Turn the buns out on to a cooling rack and place another cooling rack or a clean oven shelf on top of the buns and turn them right side up again. Using a pastry brush, paint each bun very generously with the topping. It will look far too thick when it first goes on but the warmth from the bun soon evens it out.

BREADMAKER TIPS
To make the dough, put the liquid ingredients in first, then the dry ingredients, adding the yeast last. Use the Dough programme to mix the dough and allow it to rise. Leave it in the breadmaker for an extra 30 minutes to continue to rise, then remove from the breadmaker and continue from step 5, but have the oats toasted as at step 4 before removing the dough from the machine.

Peanut Butter and Birdseed Swirls

According to my husband, Roger, these are really good. But he did add, 'don't ask me what's in them!'. The answer, of course, is a delicious and very healthy combination of pumpkin, sunflower and sesame seeds with raisins, peanut butter and muscovado sugar – absolutely delicious!

MAKES 15 BUNS

FOR THE DOUGH
565 g/1 lb 4 oz strong white bread flour
200 g/7 oz porridge oats
10 g/2 tsp salt
30 g/1 oz dark muscovado sugar
1/2 tsp freshly grated nutmeg
2 sachets + 1 tsp easy-blend dried yeast

50 g/1³/₄ oz honey
100 g/3¹/₂ oz butter, melted
1 egg, beaten
330 g/11¹/₂ oz warm water
FOR THE FILLING
50 g/1³/₄ oz pumpkin seeds
60 g/2 oz sunflower seeds
45 g/1²/₃ oz sesame seeds
100 g/3¹/₂ oz raisins

100 g/3¹/₂ oz dark muscovado sugar
280 g/10 oz smooth or crunchy peanut butter, warmed
20 g/³/₄ oz vegetable or sunflower oil, for brushing
FOR THE TOPPING
115 g/4 oz clear honey or golden (light corn) syrup, slightly warmed

1   Place all the dough ingredients in your mixer bowl and combine with the dough hook on speed 1 for 2 minutes until you have a soft dough that doesn't smear the bottom of the bowl. You may need to add a little flour or warm water, no more than 15 g/¹/₂ oz at a time, to get the desired consistency.

2   Mix on speed 2 for 5 minutes. Add another 15 g/¹/₂ oz of warm water to ensure you have a soft dough, then continue to mix on speed 2 for a further 5 minutes. Keep an eye on the consistency throughout; better a bit too soft than adding too much flour. The oats soak up a lot of water throughout the mixing.

3   Take the dough out of the mixer, knead it a few times and mould it into a head (see page 14). Place it back in the mixing bowl, cover with clingfilm (plastic wrap) and a tea towel (dish cloth) and leave to rise for 1¹/₂ hours or until doubled in size.

4   Meanwhile, toast the pumpkin and sunflower seeds in a preheated oven at 180°C/350°F/gas 4/fan oven 160°C for 5 minutes. Remove from the oven and allow to cool. Toss the sesame seeds in a dry frying pan (skillet) for a minute or two until lightly golden, then tip out of the pan immediately into a bowl to prevent them burning.

5   Knock the dough back, knead it a few times and reshape it into a head. Re-cover and allow to rest for 10 minutes. Grease and flour a 33 x 23 cm/13 x 9 in baking tin (pan). Then combine the toasted seeds with the remaining filling ingredients except the peanut butter in a small bowl.

6   Roll the head of dough into a fat sausage (see page 20), then gently mush the dough down evenly so you can begin rolling it into a rectangle. Roll out the dough into a 68 x 43 cm/27 x 17 in rectangle (see pages 21–22). Gently spread the peanut butter evenly all over the dough, to the very edges, but leave a 2.5 cm/1 in uncovered border along the bottom of the longer edge. Sprinkle the remaining filling ingredients evenly on top of the peanut butter. Dampen the border with water using your fingertips to seal the dough when you finish rolling it up.

7   Starting at the top of the long covered edge, begin to curl the edge over on to the dough, working towards you. Try to make this first curl small and close as this will be the centre of your buns. Then carefully and slowly roll the dough towards you, trying to keep the forming sausage the same thickness. If the ends are becoming too short, you can gently stretch them to fit.

8   You are aiming to get a 76 cm/30 in long sausage so, starting with your hands in the middle, gently roll the sausage and work your hands slowly from the middle towards the outside edges as you roll. If the ends of the sausage are really ragged or very thin, just trim these off a little with a knife.

9   When it is the right length, brush the entire sausage with the oil (this will enable you to separate the rolls after they are baked).

10   Using a ruler, mark off three 25 cm/10 in sections by pressing gently with a knife. Then, within each of these sections, mark at 5 cm/2 in intervals so you end up with five sections from each 25 cm/10 in section, or 15 sections in all. Using a sawing (not cutting) action with a large serrated knife, cut through each of the marks. Place the buns spiral-side up in the prepared pan in five rows of three buns each.

11   Cover the pan with clingfilm and a tea towel and allow the buns to rise for 45 minutes.

12   About 15 minutes before the end of the rising time, preheat the oven to 180°C/350°F/gas 4/fan oven 160°C.

13   Bake on the middle oven shelf for 30–33 minutes until lightly golden. Turn the buns out on to a cooling rack and place another cooling rack or a clean oven shelf on top of the buns and turn them right side up again. Using a pastry brush, paint each bun very generously with the warm honey or golden syrup.

BREADMAKER TIPS
To make the dough, put the liquid ingredients in first, then the dry ingredients, adding the yeast last. Use the Dough programme to mix the dough and allow it to rise. Leave it in the breadmaker for an extra 30 minutes to continue to rise, then remove from the breadmaker and continue from step 4.

Chocolate Bars

I've heard about people who eat their chocolate bars between two slices of bread and this is my take on the idea. If you don't have mini loaf tins, these should also work in ramekins (custard cups). In a breadmaker you can use the Dough programme then continue from step 5. See photograph on page 5.

MAKES 8 INDIVIDUAL LOAVES

FOR THE DOUGH
500 g/1 lb 2 oz strong white bread flour

5 g/1 tsp salt
5 g/1 tsp caster (superfine) sugar
1 sachet of easy-blend dried yeast
15 g/½ oz butter, melted

300 g/10½ oz warm water
FOR THE FILLING
200 g/7 oz plain (semi-sweet) chocolate

1 Place all the dough ingredients in your mixer bowl and combine with the dough hook on speed 1 for 2 minutes until you have a soft dough that doesn't smear the bottom of the bowl. You may need to add a little flour or warm water, no more than 15 g/½ oz at a time, to get the desired consistency.

2 Mix on speed 2 for 10 minutes and check frequently to maintain a soft dough that isn't smearing the bottom.

3 Take the dough out of the mixer, knead it a few times and mould it into a head (see page 14). Place it back in the mixing bowl, cover with clingfilm (plastic wrap) and a tea towel (dish cloth) and leave to rise for 30 minutes.

4 Knock back the dough, mould it back into a head, re-cover and leave to rise for a further 30 minutes or until doubled in size.

5 Divide the dough into eight 100 g/3½ oz portions and share around any leftover dough equally between the portions. Mould the portions round (see pages 16–17), then cover and leave to rest for 5 minutes.

6 Meanwhile, grease and flour eight mini loaf tins (pans). Place them all on a solid baking (cookie) sheet. Cut the chocolate into thin bars or small squares.

7 Roll out each portion to a 15 cm/6 in round (see pages 18–19), keeping the finished rounds covered as you work on the others.

8 Lay out all the rounds and share out the chocolate equally in neat horizontal lines between them, placing them close to the top of each round.

9 Take the top edge of one of the rounds and fold it over the chocolate. Then continue rolling and stop when the seam is on the bottom.

10 Pick up the roll, fold both ends in towards the bottom and place it in a prepared tin. Repeat with the remaining rounds.

11 Give the loaves a very light dusting of flour, then cover lightly with clingfilm and a tea towel and leave to rise for 30 minutes.

12 About 15 minutes before the end of the rising time, preheat the oven to 220°C/425°F/gas 7/fan oven 200°C.

13 Bake for 15–18 minutes or until the loaves are a light golden colour, then transfer to a wire rack to cool.

PIZZA

I always remember as a kid going out to dinner and being very impressed by rectangular Sicilian pizza. I like my solid baking (cookie) sheet better than my flimsy round pizza tin, so I now make rectangular – well almost square – pizzas.

Pizza at our house usually happens from a Thursday onwards, made from any fresh stuff left in the fridge plus things from the storecupboard. The dough will give you a good bready pizza base without being heavy or stodgy. I roll out the dough and place it on the sheet to give it the 20 minutes it needs to rise while I prepare the sauce and the topping ingredients.

Do be inventive and create your own pizza toppings – just be aware that overly wet toppings and overloading the base will give you a stodgy, soggy crust.

Bacon and Cheddar Pizza

You can make one large pizza or make smaller ones, if you prefer, and go for the traditional round shape, or the rectangular shape that I prefer – which is actually how the Spaniards make their 'pizzas'. But then I like the crunchy corners. This is not an Italian style, of course, but I think it tastes great.

MAKES 1 LARGE PIZZA

FOR THE DOUGH
450 g/1 lb strong white bread flour
5 g/1 tsp caster (superfine) sugar
10 g/2 tsp salt
1 sachet of easy-blend dried yeast
15 g/$^1/_2$ oz extra virgin olive oil
260 g/9$^1/_2$ oz warm water

Cornmeal, for sprinkling
FOR THE SAUCE
70 g/2$^1/_2$ oz tomato purée (paste)
75 g/2$^2/_3$ oz water
2 anchovies, very finely chopped
1 garlic clove, crushed
A pinch of caster sugar
1 tsp dried basil
15 g/$^1/_2$ oz extra virgin olive oil

Salt and freshly ground black pepper
FOR THE TOPPING
1 onion, finely chopped
200 g/7 oz grated mature Cheddar cheese
4 or 5 rashers (slices) of smoked streaky bacon, chopped
30 g/1 oz sliced black olives
1 tsp dried basil
15 g/$^1/_2$ oz extra virgin olive oil

1   Place all the dough ingredients in your mixer bowl and combine with the dough hook on speed 1 for 2 minutes until you have a soft dough that doesn't smear the bottom of the bowl. You may need to add a little flour or warm water, no more than 15 g/$^1/_2$ oz at a time, to get the desired consistency.

2   Mix on speed 2 for 10 minutes. Keep an eye on the consistency throughout; better a bit too soft than adding too much flour.

3   Take the dough out of the mixer, knead it a few times and mould it into a head (see page 14). Place it back in the mixing bowl, cover with clingfilm (plastic wrap) and a tea towel (dish cloth) and leave to rise for 1 hour.

4   Knock the dough back, take it out of the mixing bowl and mould it back into a head. Re-cover and allow to rest for 10 minutes.

5   Grease and flour a 33 x 30 cm/13 x 12 in baking (cookie) sheet or just line with non-stick liner. Sprinkle the sheet lightly with cornmeal.

6 Roll out the dough to a 30 x 28 cm/12 x 11 in rectangle (see pages 21–2) and place it on the baking sheet. The dough now needs to rest for a good 20 minutes before baking, but you can top the pizza base towards the end of this time.

7 Preheat the oven to 220°C/425°F/gas 7/fan oven 200°C.

8 Meanwhile, mix together all the sauce ingredients. Spread the sauce evenly over the base leaving a 2.5 cm/1 in border all around the outside edge.

9 Sprinkle the onion evenly over the sauce. Follow with the cheese, then the bacon and the olives. Sprinkle the entire pizza with the dried basil and add a good grinding of black pepper. Drizzle with the extra virgin olive oil.

10 Bake for 20–25 minutes until the crust is risen and golden and the topping is cooked. Place any 'second round' slices on a wire cooling rack so the base doesn't go soggy.

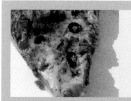

BREADMAKER TIPS
To make the dough, put the liquid ingredients in first, then the dry ingredients, adding the yeast last. Use the Dough programme to mix the dough and allow it to rise, then remove from the breadmaker and continue from step 4.

Maple Cured Bacon Pizza

I had some maple-cured bacon left over from another meal and I thought the sweet bacon would go really well with mild flavour of Mozzarella so I started to experiment. I think the combination is delicious. In a breadmaker, you can use the Dough programme then continue from step 2.

MAKES 1 LARGE PIZZA

1 quantity of Pizza Dough (see page 112)
Cornmeal, for sprinkling
FOR THE SAUCE
70 g/2½ oz tomato purée (paste)
75 g/2⅔ oz water
A pinch of caster sugar

1 tsp dried basil
A few springs of fresh thyme or a pinch of dried
15 g/½ oz extra virgin olive oil
A few drops of Tabasco sauce
Salt and freshly ground black pepper
FOR THE TOPPING
1 onion, finely chopped

200 g/7 oz Mozzarella cheese, grated
4 rashers (slices) of maple cured back bacon, chopped
1 tsp dried basil
A few sprigs of fresh thyme or a pinch of dried
15 g/½ oz extra virgin olive oil

1   Prepare the dough as for Bacon and Cheddar Pizza steps 1–3 (see page 112).

2   Knock the dough back, take it out of the mixing bowl and mould it back into a head. Re-cover and allow to rest for 10 minutes.

3   Grease and flour a 33 x 30 cm/13 x 12 in baking (cookie) sheet or just line with non-stick liner. Sprinkle the sheet lightly with cornmeal.

4   Roll out the dough to a 30 x 28 cm/12 x 11 in rectangle (see pages 21–2) and place it on the baking sheet. The dough now needs to rest for a good 20 minutes before baking, but you can top the pizza base towards the end of this time.

5   Preheat the oven to 220°C/425°F/gas 7/fan oven 200°C.

6   Meanwhile, mix together all the sauce ingredients. Spread the sauce evenly over the base leaving a 2.5 cm/1 in border all around the outside edge.

7   Sprinkle the onion evenly over the sauce. Follow with the cheese, then the bacon. Sprinkle the entire pizza with the dried basil, the thyme and a grinding of black pepper. Drizzle with the extra virgin olive oil.

8   Bake for 20–22 minutes until the crust is risen and golden and the topping is cooked. Place any 'second round' slices on a wire cooling rack so the base doesn't go soggy.

Sausage Pizza

You can use any sausage you like for this pizza, but I like spicy ones best as they give the pizza that extra bit of kick. I have made this pizza with all kinds of sausages, but I think my favourite is a Cajun spiced sausage, which works particularly well. In a breadmaker, you can use the Dough programme, then continue from step 2.

MAKES 1 LARGE PIZZA

1 quantity of Pizza Dough (see page 112)
Cornmeal, for sprinkling
FOR THE SAUCE
70 g/2½ oz tomato purée (paste)
75 g/2⅔ oz water
2 anchovies, very finely chopped

1 garlic clove, crushed
A pinch of caster sugar
1 tbsp chopped fresh oregano
15 g/½ oz sun-dried tomato oil, from the jar
Salt and freshly ground black pepper
FOR THE TOPPING
80 g/2¾ oz canned mushrooms, sliced

1 onion, finely chopped
4 sun-dried tomatoes, chopped
200 g/7 oz Mozzarella cheese, grated
2 cooked sausages, skinned and the meat crumbled
1 tbsp chopped fresh oregano
15 g/½ oz extra virgin olive oil

1   Prepare the dough as for Bacon and Cheddar Pizza steps 1–3 (see page 112).

2   Knock the dough back, take it out of the mixing bowl and mould it back into a head. Re-cover and allow to rest for 10 minutes.

3   Grease and flour a 33 x 30 cm/13 x 12 in baking (cookie) sheet or just line with non-stick liner. Sprinkle the sheet lightly with cornmeal.

4   Roll out the dough to a 30 x 28 cm/12 x 11 in rectangle (see pages 21–2) and place it on the baking sheet. The dough now needs to rest for a good 20 minutes before baking, but you can top the pizza base towards the end of this time.

5   Preheat the oven to 220°C/425°F/gas 7/fan oven 200°C.

6   Mix together all the sauce ingredients. Spread the sauce evenly over the base leaving a 2.5 cm/1 in border all around the outside edge.

7   Drain the mushrooms and squeeze to remove excess liquid. Sprinkle the onion evenly over the sauce. Follow with the mushrooms, sun-dried tomatoes and then the cheese. Then add the crumbled sausage. Sprinkle the entire pizza with the oregano. Grind a little black pepper over the top and drizzle with the extra virgin olive oil.

8   Bake for 20–22 minutes until the crust is risen and the topping is cooked. Place any 'second round' slices on a cooling rack so the base doesn't go soggy.

Chicken Pizza

With the tomatoes, oregano and Parmesan, this pizza has a seriously Italian flavour. Delicious! This is a wonderful way to use up chicken leftover after your Sunday roast, but you can use any cooked chicken torn into pieces. In a breadmaker, you can use the Dough programme then continue from step 2.

MAKES 1 LARGE PIZZA

1 quantity of Pizza Dough (see page 112)
Cornmeal, for sprinkling
FOR THE SAUCE
40 g/1½ oz tomato purée (paste)
40 g/1½ oz water
1 small garlic clove, crushed

A pinch of sugar
½ tsp dried oregano
7.5 g/1½ tsp extra virgin olive oil
Salt and freshly ground black pepper
FOR THE TOPPING
1 onion, finely chopped
150 g/5 oz cooked chicken, in chunks
100 g/3½ oz full-fat cream cheese

30 g/1 oz sun-dried tomatoes, cut into thin strips
40 g/1½ oz double (heavy) cream
30 g/1 oz Pecorino or Parmesan cheese, grated
1 tsp dried oregano
15 g/½ oz extra virgin olive oil

1 Prepare the dough as for Bacon and Cheddar Pizza steps 1–3 (see page 112).

2 Knock the dough back, take it out of the mixing bowl and mould it back into a head. Re-cover and allow to rest for 10 minutes.

3 Grease and flour a 33 x 30 cm/13 x 12 in baking (cookie) sheet or just line with non-stick liner. Sprinkle the sheet lightly with cornmeal.

4 Roll out the dough to a 30 x 28 cm/12 x 11 in rectangle (see pages 21–2) and place it on the baking sheet. The dough now needs to rest for a good 20 minutes before baking, but you can top the pizza base towards the end of this time.

5 Preheat the oven to 220°C/425°F/gas 7/fan oven 200°C.

6 Mix together all the sauce ingredients. Spread the sauce evenly over the base leaving a 2.5 cm/1 in border all around the outside edge.

7 Sprinkle the onion evenly over the sauce. Follow with the chicken and then dollop with evenly spaced heaped teaspoonfuls of cream cheese. Place the strips of sun-dried tomato evenly over the pizza. Pour the cream evenly over. Add the Pecorino or Parmesan, the oregano, olive oil and a few grindings of black pepper.

8 Bake for 20–22 minutes until the crust is risen and the topping is cooked. Place any 'second round' slices on a cooling rack so the base doesn't go soggy.

Potato Pizza

This was inspired by Nigel Slater's potato pizza, another quite surprising combination that I feel works really well. It combines sliced potatoes with Camembert or Brie and some tasty, mature Cheddar with crème fraîche and, another of my favourites, red onion. In a breadmaker, you can use the Dough programme then continue from step 2.

MAKES 1 LARGE PIZZA

1 quantity of Pizza Dough (see page 112) but use half strong white flour and half wholemeal bread flour

Cornmeal, for sprinkling

FOR THE TOPPING

80 g/2³⁄₄ oz crème fraîche

1 red onion, halved and finely sliced

225 g/8 oz raw weight new potatoes, cooked, cooled and sliced

Salt and freshly ground black pepper

120 g/4¹⁄₄ oz Camembert or Brie, sliced

100 g/3¹⁄₂ oz grated mature Cheddar cheese

1 tbsp chopped fresh thyme

2 tbsp chopped fresh parsley

30 g/1 oz extra virgin olive oil

1　Prepare the dough as for Bacon and Cheddar Pizza steps 1–3 (see page 112).

2　Knock the dough back, take it out of the mixing bowl and mould it back into a head. Re-cover and allow to rest for 10 minutes.

3　Grease and flour a 33 x 30 cm/13 x 12 in baking (cookie) sheet or just line with non-stick liner. Sprinkle the sheet lightly with cornmeal.

4　Roll out the dough to a 30 x 28 cm/12 x 11 in rectangle (see pages 21–2) and place it on the baking sheet. The dough now needs to rest for a good 20 minutes before baking, but you can top the pizza base towards the end of this time.

5　Preheat the oven to 220°C/425°F/gas 7/fan oven 200°C.

6　Spread the crème fraîche over the pizza base leaving a 2.5 cm/1 in border all around the outside edge. Follow with the onion and the sliced potatoes. Season with salt and pepper, then add the slices of Camembert or Brie and the grated Cheddar. Add the thyme and half the parsley. Grind a little more pepper over the top and drizzle with the extra virgin olive oil.

7　Bake for 20–25 minutes until the crust is risen and the topping is cooked. Sprinkle with the remaining parsley and serve. Place any 'second round' slices on a cooling rack so the base doesn't go soggy.

Christmas Eve Pizza

Many of my pizza toppings are not really what you'd expect in an authentic Italian restaurant, but I think pizza has become a truly international dish so you can top it with whatever takes your fancy. This unusual combination really does work. Do use my cranberry sauce if you can – home-made really is best.

MAKES 1 LARGE PIZZA

FOR THE DOUGH
225 g/8 oz strong white bread flour
225 g/8 oz wholemeal bread flour
5 g/1 tsp caster (superfine) sugar
10 g/2 tsp salt

1 sachet of easy-blend dried yeast
15 g/½ oz extra virgin olive oil
265 g/scant 10 oz warm water
Cornmeal, for sprinkling
FOR THE TOPPING
80 g/2¾ oz full-fat crème fraîche
2 tbsp chopped fresh parsley

Salt and freshly ground black pepper
1 onion, finely chopped
40 g/1½ oz Stilton cheese, grated
115 g/4 oz cream cheese
130 g/4½ oz Cranberry Sauce (see opposite)
200 g/7 oz Mozzarella cheese, grated

1 Place all the dough ingredients in your mixer bowl and combine with the dough hook on speed 1 for 2 minutes until you have a soft dough that doesn't smear the bottom of the bowl. You may need to add a little flour or warm water, no more than 15 g/½ oz at a time, to get the desired consistency.

2 Mix on speed 2 for 10 minutes. Keep an eye on the consistency throughout; better a bit too soft than adding too much flour.

3 Take the dough out of the mixer, knead it a few times and mould it into a head (see page 14). Place it back in the mixing bowl, cover with clingfilm (plastic wrap) and a tea towel (dish cloth) and leave to rise for 1 hour.

4 Knock the dough back, take it out of the mixing bowl and mould it back into a head. Re-cover and allow to rest for 10 minutes.

5 Grease and flour a 33 x 30 cm/13 x 12 in baking (cookie) sheet or just line with non-stick liner. Sprinkle the sheet lightly with cornmeal.

CRANBERRY SAUCE

140 g/5 oz caster (superfine) sugar

150 g/5 oz water

225 g/8 oz fresh cranberries

1 Place the sugar and water in a saucepan. Stir over a low heat to dissolve the sugar, then bring to the boil.

2 Add the cranberries and cook for about 8–10 minutes until they pop and the sauce thickens.

3 Remove from the heat and allow to cool before adding to the pizza.

6 Roll out the dough to a 30 x 28 cm/12 x 11 in rectangle (see pages 21–2) and place it on the baking sheet. The dough now needs to rest for a good 20 minutes before baking, but you can top the pizza base towards the end of this time.

7 Preheat the oven to 220°C/425°F/gas 7/fan oven 200°C.

8 Spread the crème fraîche evenly over the base leaving a 2.5 cm/1 in border all around the outside edge.

9 Sprinkle half the parsley evenly over the crème fraîche. Sprinkle a very little salt and a grinding of black pepper over. Follow with the onion and the Stilton and then dollop with evenly spaced heaped teaspoonfuls of cream cheese. Then dollop on the cranberry sauce. Sprinkle the Mozzarella over and give it all another grinding of black pepper.

10 Bake for 20–22 minutes until the crust is risen and the topping is cooked. Sprinkle with the remaining parsley and serve. Place any 'second round' slices on a cooling rack so the base doesn't go soggy.

BREADMAKER TIPS

To make the dough, put the liquid ingredients in first, then the dry ingredients, adding the yeast last. Use the Dough programme to mix the dough and allow it to rise, then remove from the breadmaker and continue from step 4.

Seafood Pizza

I think this creamy seafood pizza is wonderful. You can either use a seafood mix or put together your own if you have particular favourites. The roasted pumpkin seed oil gives a beautiful pale green dough with a wonderful texture. In a breadmaker, you can use the Dough programme then continue from Step 4.

MAKES 1 PIZZA

1 quantity of Pizza Dough (see page 112) but use half strong white bread flour and half wholemeal bread flour

Cornmeal, for sprinkling

FOR THE TOPPING

80 g/2¾ oz crème fraîche

1 onion, halved and thinly sliced

2 tbsp chopped fresh parsley

Salt and freshly ground black pepper

200 g/7 oz cream cheese

200 g/7 oz pre-cooked seafood mix (muscles, prawns and squid)

100 g/3½ oz Mozzarella cheese, grated

15 g/½ oz pumpkin seed oil

1   Prepare the dough as for Bacon and Cheddar Pizza steps 1–3 (see page 112).

2   Knock the dough back, take it out of the mixing bowl and mould it back into a head. Re-cover and allow to rest for 10 minutes.

3   Grease and flour a 33 x 30 cm/13 x 12 in baking (cookie) sheet or just line with non-stick liner. Sprinkle the sheet lightly with cornmeal.

4   Roll out the dough to a 30 x 28 cm/12 x 11 in rectangle (see pages 21–2) and place it on the baking sheet. Leave to rest for a good 20 minutes before baking.

5   Preheat the oven to 220°C/425°F/gas 7/fan oven 200°C.

6   Spread the crème fraîche evenly over the base leaving a 2.5 cm/1 in border.

7   Sprinkle the onion evenly over the crème fraîche. Sprinkle over half the parsley and follow with a little salt and pepper. Dollop teaspoonfuls of cream cheese evenly over the pizza. Share around the seafood evenly. Sprinkle the Mozzarella over, drizzle with the pumpkin seed oil and finish with a little more salt and pepper.

8   Bake for 20–22 minutes until the crust is risen and the topping is cooked. Sprinkle with the remaining parsley and serve.

FLAT BREADS

I really like these flat breads. If it seems silly to let dough rise, mould it round and leave it to rise again – just to roll it out flat – there is a reason. During the rising time the bread is developing flavour. While it is resting after moulding round it is still developing flavour and it is also relaxing to make rolling out easier.

When the breads have just come out of the oven they are usually crisp around the edges and chewy in the middle. This is all good but, for me, these breads are at their best when reheated at 180°C/350°F/gas 4/fan oven 160°C for 5–6 minutes. When they come back out of the oven they will still be floppy but give them a minute or two and they go crisp and crunchy all over. They are perfect for scooping up dips, salsa, anything mushy or anything that needs a little help to push on to your fork.

Crunchy Peanut Butter Flat Bread

This is really good with pilaffs, stir-fries or anything that goes with the delicious peanut flavour. When the breads are warm and crunchy all over after reheating, the flavour of the peanut butter really comes through. Don't bother with a knife when you are eating flat breads – just pull them apart with your fingers.

MAKES 6 BREADS

370 g/13 oz strong white bread flour

5 g/1 tsp salt
25 g/1 oz light muscovado sugar
1 sachet of easy-blend dried yeast

80 g/2¾ oz crunchy peanut butter
210 g/7½ oz warm water

1   Place all the ingredients in your mixer bowl and combine with the dough hook on speed 1 for 2 minutes until you have a soft dough that doesn't smear the bottom of the bowl. You may need to add a little flour or warm water, no more than 15 g/½ oz at a time, to get the desired consistency.

2   Mix on speed 2 for 10 minutes. Keep an eye on the consistency throughout; better a bit too soft than adding too much flour.

3   Take the dough out of the mixer, knead it a few times and mould it into a head (see page 14). Place it back in the mixing bowl, cover with clingfilm (plastic wrap) and a tea towel (dish cloth) and leave to rise for 1 hour (it won't rise much).

4   Knock the dough back, take it out of the mixing bowl and mould it back into a head. Re-cover and allow to rest for 10 minutes.

5   Divide the dough into six 115 g/4 oz portions and share around any leftover dough equally between the portions. Mould round (see pages 16–17) and place the portions about 5 cm/2 in apart on a baking (cookie) sheet or just leave them on the work surface. Cover with clingfilm and a tea towel and leave to rest for 45 minutes.

6 About 15 minutes before the end of the resting time, place the oven shelves one at the very bottom and another at the very top of the oven and preheat the oven to 220°C/425°F/gas 7/fan oven 200°C. Ideally prepare three baking sheets by greasing and flouring them or lining with non-stick lining, but two sheets will do – or even one if you are patient.

7 Using a little bread flour for dusting, roll out one of the portions to a 30 x 20 cm/12 x 8 in oval. The size and shape doesn't need to be perfect; the point is to roll it out nice and thin and as long as you get the bread to about these dimensions you're fine.

8 Carefully lift the bread, supporting it with both hands to avoid stretching, and lay it on one of the baking sheets. Prick it with a fork seven times.

9 Place the sheet on the bottom oven shelf and set the timer for 3½ minutes. Meanwhile, roll out another portion, place it on the second sheet and prick it with a fork seven times.

10 When the 3½ minutes is up, move the first sheet to the top shelf and place the second sheet on the bottom. Set the timer for 3½ minutes again.

11 Roll out another portion, place it on the third sheet and prick it as before.

12 When the first bread is finished, transfer it to a wire rack to cool and move the second sheet to the top oven shelf and put the third sheet on the bottom. Start again with the first sheet and continue until all six flat breads are baked. You can pile up the finished flat breads on one rack – no problem.

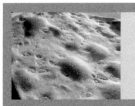

BREADMAKER TIPS
To make the dough, put the liquid ingredients in first, then the dry ingredients, adding the yeast last. Use the Dough programme to mix the dough and allow it to rise, then remove from the breadmaker and continue from step 4.

Toasted Hazelnut and Nutella Flat Bread

This bread is more about hazelnuts than chocolate – which you may be surprised to learn, knowing how much I love chocolate! The colour is subtle and the flavour is absolutely delicious. You can serve it as a sweet snack, and it works really well as a breakfast bread just as it is.

MAKES 7 BREADS

FOR THE DOUGH
435 g/15½ oz strong white bread flour
10 g/2 tsp salt

25 g/1 oz light muscovado sugar
1 sachet of easy-blend dried yeast
40 g/1½ oz Nutella chocolate and hazelnut (filbert) spread
60 g/2 oz butter, melted

210 g/½ oz warm water
FOR THE FILLING
50 g/1¾ oz hazelnuts

1 Place all the dough ingredients in your mixer bowl and combine with the dough hook on speed 1 for 2 minutes until you have a soft dough that doesn't smear the bottom of the bowl. You may need to add a little flour or warm water, no more than 15 g/½ oz at a time, to get the desired consistency.

2 Mix on speed 2 for 10 minutes, adding a little bread flour if necessary to maintain the correct dough consistency.

3 Take the dough out of the mixer, knead it a few times and mould it into a head (see page 14). Place it back in the mixing bowl, cover with clingfilm (plastic wrap) and a tea towel (dish cloth) and leave to rise for 1 hour (it won't rise much).

4 Meanwhile, preheat the oven to 180°C/350°F/gas 4/fan oven 160°C. Place the whole hazelnuts on a baking (cooking) sheet and toast them in the oven for 7–8 minutes. Turn off the oven and remove the nuts. Allow them to cool a bit, then chop them finely.

5 Lay the risen dough on to your work surface and flatten it out a bit. Place the chopped hazelnuts on top and fold the dough over to enclose the nuts. Using your metal scraper, chop the nuts into the dough (see page 23).

6 Divide the dough into seven 115 g/4 oz portions and share around any leftover dough equally between the portions. Mould round (see pages 16–17) and place the portions about 5 cm/2 in apart on the baking sheet. Cover with clingfilm and a tea towel and leave to rest for 45 minutes.

7 About 15 minutes before the end of the resting time, place the oven shelves one at the very bottom and another at the very top of the oven and preheat the oven to 220°C/425°F/gas 7/fan oven 200°C. Ideally prepare three baking sheets by greasing and flouring them or lining with non-stick lining, but two sheets will do – or even one if you are patient.

8 Using a little bread flour for dusting, roll out one of the portions to a 30 x 20 cm/12 x 8 in oval. The size and shape doesn't need to be perfect; the point is to roll it out nice and thin and as long as you get the bread to about these dimensions you're fine.

9 Carefully lift the bread, supporting it with both hands to avoid stretching, and lay it on one of the baking sheets. Prick it with a fork seven times.

10 Place the sheet on the bottom oven shelf and set the timer for 3½ minutes. Meanwhile, roll out another portion, place it on the second sheet and prick it with a fork seven times.

11 When the 3½ minutes is up, move the first sheet to the top shelf and place the second sheet on the bottom. Set the timer for 3½ minutes again.

12 Roll out another portion, place it on the third sheet and prick it as before.

13 When the first bread is finished, transfer it to a wire rack to cool and move the second sheet to the top oven shelf and put the third sheet on the bottom. Start again with the first sheet and continue until all seven flat breads are baked.

BREADMAKER TIPS
To make the dough, put the liquid ingredients in first, then the dry ingredients, adding the yeast last. Use the Dough programme to mix the dough and allow it to rise, then remove from the breadmaker and continue from step 4.

Tahini Flat Bread

These are very moreish! I love to serve them with spicy dishes or pulses and a fresh mixed salad, but they go with pretty much anything with their wonderful sesame flavour. All in all, they are wonderfully versatile flatbreads and a great standby to have in the freezer for when unexpected guests turn up for a drink and a nibble.

MAKES 6 BREADS

50 g/1³/₄ oz sesame seeds

415 g/14¹/₂ oz strong white bread flour
10 g/2 tsp salt
25 g/1 oz light muscovado sugar

80 g/2³/₄ oz tahini paste
1 sachet of easy-blend dried yeast
210 g/7¹/₂ oz warm water

1   Toss the sesame seeds in a dry frying pan (skillet) until golden. Keep the seeds moving in the pan or they will burn easily. Tip on to a plate immediately and allow to cool.

2   Place the sesame seeds and all the remaining ingredients in your mixer bowl and combine with the dough hook on speed 1 for 2 minutes until you have a soft dough that doesn't smear the bottom of the bowl. You may need to add a little flour or warm water, no more than 15 g/¹/₂ oz at a time, to get the desired consistency.

3   Mix on speed 2 for 10 minutes. You may need to add a little more flour but too soft is better than making the dough stiff with too much extra.

4   Take the dough out of the mixer, knead it a few times and mould it into a head (see page 14). Place it back in the mixing bowl, cover with clingfilm (plastic wrap) and a tea towel (dish cloth) and leave to rise for 1 hour (it won't rise much).

5   Knock the dough back, take it out of the mixing bowl and mould it back into a head. Re-cover and allow to rest for 10 minutes.

6   Divide the dough into six 115 g/4 oz portions and share around any leftover dough equally between the portions. Mould round (see pages

16–17) and place the portions about 5 cm/2 in apart on a baking (cookie) sheet. Cover with clingfilm and a tea towel and leave to rest for 45 minutes.

7 About 15 minutes before the end of the resting time, place the oven shelves one at the very bottom and another at the very top of the oven and preheat the oven to 220°C/425°F/gas 7/fan oven 200°C. Ideally prepare three baking sheets by greasing and flouring them or lining with non-stick lining, but two sheets will do – or even one if you are patient.

8 Using a little bread flour for dusting, roll out one of the portions to a 30 x 20 cm/12 x 8 in oval. The size and shape doesn't need to be perfect; the point is to roll it out nice and thin and as long as you get the bread to about these dimensions you're fine.

9 Carefully lift the bread, supporting it with both hands to avoid stretching, and lay it on one of the baking sheets. Prick it with a fork seven times.

10 Place the sheet on the bottom oven shelf and set the timer for 3½ minutes. Meanwhile, roll out another portion, place it on the second sheet and prick it with a fork. seven times

11 When the 3½ minutes is up, move the first sheet to the top shelf and place the second sheet on the bottom. Set the timer for 3½ minutes again.

12 Roll out another portion, place it on the third sheet and prick it as before.

13 When the first bread is finished, transfer it to a wire rack to cool and move the second sheet to the top oven shelf and put the third sheet on the bottom. Start again with the first sheet and continue until all six flat breads are baked.

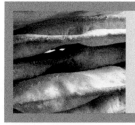

BREADMAKER TIPS
To make the dough, put the liquid ingredients in first, then the dry ingredients, adding the yeast last. Use the Dough programme to mix the dough and allow it to rise, then remove from the breadmaker and continue from step 5. Toast the sesame seeds as at step 1 before you begin.

Pumpkin Seed Flat Bread

This is one of my favourite breads, with its beautiful colour from the pumpkin seed oil, and just a delicate hint of sweetness from the muscovado sugar. I love it reheated and all crunchy from the oven, served on its own or as a side dish with grilled meats. Think about making some of these next time you fire up the barbecue!

MAKES 7 BREADS

FOR THE DOUGH
415 g/14½ oz strong white bread flour

10 g/2 tsp salt
25 g/1 oz light muscovado sugar
1 sachet of easy-blend dried yeast
80 g/2¾ oz roasted pumpkin seed oil

200 g/7 oz warm water
FOR THE FILLING
70 g/2½ oz pumpkin seeds

1. Place all the dough ingredients in your mixer bowl and combine with the dough hook on speed 1 for 2 minutes until you have a soft dough that doesn't smear the bottom of the bowl. You may need to add a little flour or warm water, no more than 15 g/½ oz at a time, to get the desired consistency.

2. Mix on speed 2 for 10 minutes. You may need to add a little more flour but too soft is better than making the dough stiff with too much extra.

3. Take the dough out of the mixer, knead it a few times and mould it into a head (see page 14). Place it back in the mixing bowl, cover with clingfilm (plastic wrap) and a tea towel (dish cloth) and leave to rise for 1 hour (it won't rise much).

4. Meanwhile, preheat the oven to 180°C/350°F/ gas 4/fan oven 160°C. Put the pumpkin seeds on a baking (cookie) sheet and toast in the oven for 7–8 minutes.

5. Take the dough out of the mixing bowl and press it out flat to about 2.5 cm/1 in thick. Put the pumpkin seeds on top and, using your metal scraper, chop them into the dough (see page 23).

6 Divide the dough into seven 115 g/4 oz portions and share around any leftover dough equally between the portions. Mould round (see pages 16–17); they will lose lots of seeds but don't worry; just pat the bottom of the moulded ball on to the loose seeds to pick them up. Place the portions about 5 cm/2 in apart on the baking sheet, cover with clingfilm and a tea towel and leave to rest for 45 minutes. Again, the dough won't rise much but it needs lots of time so it is easier to roll out thinly.

7 About 15 minutes before the end of the resting time, place the oven shelves one at the very bottom and another at the very top of the oven and preheat the oven to 220°C/425°F/gas 7/fan oven 200°C. Ideally prepare three baking sheets by greasing and flouring them or lining with non-stick lining, but two sheets will do – or even one if you are patient.

8 Using a little bread flour for dusting, roll out one of the portions to a 30 x 20 cm/12 x 8 in oval. The size and shape doesn't need to be perfect; the point is to roll it out nice and thin and as long as you get the bread to about these dimensions you're fine.

9 Carefully lift the bread, supporting it with both hands to avoid stretching, and lay it on one of the baking sheets. Prick it with a fork seven times.

10 Place the sheet on the bottom oven shelf and set the timer for 3½ minutes. Meanwhile, roll out another portion, place it on the second sheet and prick it with a fork seven times.

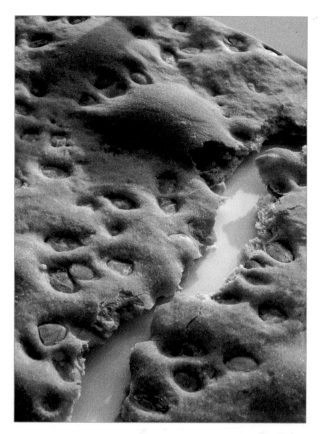

11 When the 3½ minutes is up, move the first sheet to the top shelf and place the second sheet on the bottom. Set the timer for 3½ minutes again.

12 Roll out another portion, place it on the third sheet and prick it as before.

13 When the first bread is finished, transfer it to a wire rack to cool and move the second sheet to the top oven shelf and put the third sheet on the bottom. Start again with the first sheet and continue until all seven flat breads are baked.

BREADMAKER TIPS
To make the dough, put the liquid ingredients in first, then the dry ingredients, adding the yeast last. Use the Dough programme to mix the dough and allow it to rise, then remove from the breadmaker and continue from step 4.

Chocolate Chip and Marshmallow Flat Bread

Okay, so these are frivolous and perhaps a little silly – but they taste great! Chocolate bread, toasted marshmallow and melting chocolate chips. Ahhh, chocolate lunch! Or they are perfect for a winter evening on the settee in front of an old film on the television and with a log fire crackling in the hearth.

MAKES 7 BREADS

FOR THE DOUGH
400 g/14 oz strong white bread flour
45 g/1²/₃ oz cocoa (unsweetened chocolate) powder

5 g/1 tsp salt
25 g/1 oz light muscovado sugar
80 g/2³/₄ oz unsalted butter, melted
1 sachet of easy-blend dried yeast
5 g/1 tsp vanilla essence (extract)
210 g/7¹/₂ oz warm water

50 g/1³/₄ oz melted unsalted butter, for brushing
FOR THE TOPPING
70 g/2¹/₂ oz mini marshmallows
70 g/2¹/₂ oz plain (semi-sweet) chocolate chips

1   Place all the dough ingredients in your mixer bowl and combine with the dough hook on speed 1 for 2 minutes until you have a soft dough that doesn't smear the bottom of the bowl. You may need to add a little warm water to get the desired consistency.

2   Mix on speed 2 for 10 minutes. If necessary, add a little bread flour to maintain the correct consistency.

3   Take the dough out of the mixer, knead it a few times and mould it into a head (see page 14). Place it back in the mixing bowl, cover with clingfilm (plastic wrap) and a tea towel (dish cloth) and leave to rise for 1 hour (it won't rise much).

4   Divide the dough into seven 110 g/4 oz portions and share around any leftover dough equally between the portions. Mould round (see pages 16–17). Place the portions about 5 cm/2 in apart on a baking (cookie) sheet, cover with clingfilm and a tea towel and leave to rest for 45 minutes.

5   About 15 minutes before the end of the resting time, place the oven shelves one at the very bottom and another at the very top of the oven

and preheat the oven to 220°C/425°F/gas 7/fan oven 200°C. Ideally prepare three baking sheets by greasing and flouring them or lining with non-stick lining, but two sheets will do – or even one if you are patient.

6   Using a little bread flour for dusting, roll out one of the portions to a 30 x 20 cm/12 x 8 in oval. The size and shape doesn't need to be perfect; the point is to roll it out nice and thin and as long as you get the bread to about these dimensions you're fine.

7   Carefully lift the bread, supporting it with both hands to avoid stretching, and lay it on one of the baking sheets. Using a pastry brush, brush the dough with the melted butter.

8   Prick the bread seven times with a fork. Sprinkle the bread with 10 g/2 tsp of the marshmallows and 10 g/2 tsp of the chocolate chips.

9   Place the sheet on the bottom oven shelf and set the timer for 3½ minutes. Meanwhile, roll out another portion, place it on the second sheet, prick it with a fork seven times, brush with melted butter and sprinkle with the marshmallows and chocolate chips.

10 When the 3½ minutes is up, move the first sheet to the top shelf and place the second sheet on the bottom. Set the timer for 3½ minutes again.

11 Roll out another portion, place it on the third sheet and prick it, brush with melted butter and top as before.

12 When the first bread is finished, transfer it to a wire rack to cool and move the second sheet to the top oven shelf and put the third sheet on the bottom. Start again with the first sheet and continue until all seven flat breads are baked.

BREADMAKER TIPS

To make the dough, put the liquid ingredients in first, then the dry ingredients, adding the yeast last. Use the Dough programme to mix the dough and allow it to rise, then remove from the breadmaker and continue from step 4.

Yoghurt and Herb Flat Bread

This is a good bread to make when the herb garden gets out of control so you could try other herb mixtures. In a breadmaker, you can use the Dough programme and continue from step 4. See photograph on page 121.

MAKES 7 BREADS

FOR THE DOUGH
500 g/1 lb 2 oz strong white bread flour
10 g/2 tsp salt

25 g/1 oz caster (superfine) sugar
1 sachet of easy-blend dried yeast
185 g/6½ oz yoghurt, warmed to
lukewarm
30 g/1 oz olive oil

130 g/4½ oz warm water
FOR THE FILLING
40 g/1½ oz fresh mixed herbs
FOR THE TOPPING
50 g/1¾ oz olive oil

1 Combine all the dough ingredients with the dough hook on speed 1 for 2 minutes until you have a soft dough that doesn't smear the bottom of the bowl. If it is just a little smeary, don't add any more warm water but let it stay that way as it will absorb during the 10-minute mix.

2 Mix on speed 2 for 10 minutes, keeping an eye on the dough consistency.

3 Knead the dough a few times and mould it into a head (see page 14). Place it back in the mixing bowl, cover with clingfilm (plastic wrap) and a tea towel (dish cloth) and leave to rise for 1 hour.

4 Meanwhile, wash and dry the herbs. Chop them roughly and mix them all together.

5 Spread the dough out a bit on your work surface. Place the herbs all over the surface, then wrap the dough over the herbs. Using your metal scraper, chop them into the dough (see page 23).

6 Divide the dough into seven 120 g/4¼ oz portions and share any leftover dough equally between them. Mould round (see pages 16–17). Place the portions about 5 cm/2 in apart on a baking (cookie) sheet, cover with clingfilm and a tea towel and leave to rest for 45 minutes.

7 Place the oven shelves one at the very bottom and another at the very top of the oven and preheat the oven to 220°C/425°F/gas 7/fan oven 200°C. Prepare three baking sheets by greasing and flouring them or lining with non-stick lining.

8 Using a little bread flour for dusting, roll out one of the portions to a 30 x 20 cm/12 x 8 in oval. The size and shape doesn't need to be perfect as long as you get the bread to about these dimensions.

9 Carefully lift the bread, supporting it with both hands to avoid stretching, and lay it on one of the baking sheets. Prick it with a fork seven times and brush with olive oil.

10 Place the sheet on the bottom oven shelf and set the timer for 3½ minutes. Roll out another portion, place it on the second sheet and prick it and brush it as before.

11 When the 3½ minutes is up, move the first sheet to the top shelf and place the second sheet on the bottom. Set the timer for 3½ minutes again.

12 Roll out another portion, place it on the third sheet and prick it and brush it as before.

13 When the first bread is finished, transfer it to a wire rack to cool and move the second sheet on the top oven shelf and put the third sheet on the bottom. Start again with the first sheet and continue until all seven flat breads are baked.

FANCY BAKES

This section contains all kinds of breads and loaves made with baking powder and bicarbonate of soda (baking soda) rather than yeast, from Lager Cornbread (see page 138) to banana breads and delicious doughnuts. You may like to experiment with these when you don't have much time, as obviously they are quicker to prepare and make – although no less delicious.

They are not suitable for your breadmaker unless you have a cake programme, in which case follow your manufacturer's instructions.

'Bake'

I adapted these from a recipe for roti sada, *something between a naan and a roti, my sister-in-law sent from Trinidad, but my husband Roger gleefully greeted them with 'It's Bake!', which he had eaten with cheese as a child. Easy to make, delicious as sandwiches or with curries, soups and casseroles, they also freeze well.*

MAKES 8 BREADS

480 g/1 lb 1 oz plain (all-purpose) flour

20 g/³⁄₄ oz baking powder
10 g/2 tsp salt
300 g/10¹⁄₂ oz plain yoghurt

70 g/2¹⁄₂ oz water

1   Sift the flour, baking powder and salt into a large bowl and stir thoroughly.

2   Make a well in the centre and pour in the yoghurt and water. Stir together as much as you can with a wooden spoon. It gets harder to work the wet ingredients through so, when I can't stir any more, I start making cutting motions with my spoon so I can continue bringing the mixture to a dough. It should form a heap of rough bits of dryish dough.

3   Tip the rough heap on to a work surface and finish bringing the ingredients together by kneading with your hands. As you knead the dough will get wetter, so don't add any more water, even though it looks at first as though it needs it. You may even need a light dusting of flour to finish kneading

4   Knead for about 2 minutes. The dough won't be smooth like bread dough but it will be soft and pliable and have some spring to it when you poke it with your finger after you have moulded it into a head.

5   Mould into a head (see page 14), sprinkle a little flour on the work surface, place the dough on top and cover. I cover mine with the up-turned bowl I mixed up the dough in but you can use clingfilm (plastic wrap) and a tea towel (dish cloth) if you prefer. Leave the dough to rest for 30 minutes.

6   Divide the dough into eight 110 g/4 oz portions and share around any leftover dough equally between the portions. Mould round (see pages 16–17). The dough has a sticky texture but try to use as little flour as possible; you won't be able to mould round if there is too much flour because the dough will just slip on the work surface.
Re-cover and allow to rest for 30 minutes.

7   Meanwhile, heat your griddle or a heavy frying pan (skillet) to a medium-low heat (my cooker has heat options 1–6 and I use 3 for cooking Bake).

8   Roll out a couple of portions to 18 cm/7 in rounds (see pages 18–19). You can use flour as needed here!

9   Place one of the rounds on the preheated, ungreased griddle or pan and bake for 1 minute on each side – use a timer because they shouldn't be overcooked. As the first side cooks, you will see lots of bubbles forming on top. When you turn the Bake over, don't mush it down on the griddle – there's no need too. The finished first side will have small brown spots and when you've finished the second side, it will have large brown spots where the bubbles were.

10   Transfer the finished Bake to a cooling rack and cook the second one, rolling out the remaining portions in the meantime. Carry on cooking and rolling (you really do need that timer!) until all the portions are cooked.

11   The finished Bakes can be stacked on the cooling rack or wrapped in a tea towel to keep them soft.

NOTE
If you wish, you can roll out the dough to 23 cm/9 in to use when cooked as you would tortillas. Cook them for just 30 seconds on each side.

Pumpkin Bake

Mmmm ... warm and spicy! The soft texture of the finished bread marries so well with those exotic spices. This is delicious on winter evenings and perfect for Halloween or bonfire celebrations. The prepared pumpkin purée freezes very well but, before using it, you should pour away any excess liquid that comes out as it defrosts.

MAKES 8 BREADS

FOR THE PUMPKIN PURÉE
900 g/2 lb pumpkin (squash)
440 g/15½ oz plain (all-purpose) flour

20 g/¾ oz baking powder
5 g/1 tsp salt
7.5 g/1½ tsp ground cinnamon
½ tsp ground ginger
¼ tsp grated nutmeg

¼ tsp ground allspice
⅛ tsp ground cloves
100 g/3½ oz dark muscovado sugar
70 g/2½ oz milk

1   Cut the pumpkin flesh into 5 cm/2 in chunks and steam for 35–40 minutes until tender. Purée in a food processor, then transfer to a sieve (strainer) set over a bowl and allow the excess moisture to drain from the puréed pumpkin. This will take about 2 hours. Make sure the purée is at room temperature before adding it to the rest of the ingredients when you start making the dough.

2   Sift the flour, baking powder, salt and all the spices into a large bowl and stir thoroughly.

3   Combine 300 g/10½ oz of the pumpkin purée, sugar and milk in a small bowl and mix together thoroughly with a fork.

4   Make a well in the centre of the flour and pour in the pumpkin mixture. Stir together as much as you can with a wooden spoon. When I can't stir any more, I start making cutting motions with my spoon so I can continue bringing the mixture to a dough. It should form a heap of rough bits of dough.

5   Tip the rough heap on to a work surface and finish bringing the ingredients together by kneading with your hands. As you knead the dough will get wetter, so don't add any more water, even though it looks at first as though it

needs it. You may even need a light dusting of flour to finish kneading

6 Knead for about 1 minute. The dough won't be smooth like bread dough but it will be soft and pliable and have some spring to it when you poke it with your finger after you have moulded it into a head.

7 Mould into a head (see page 14), sprinkle a little flour in the work surface, place the dough on top and cover. I cover mine with the up-turned bowl I mixed up the dough in but you can use clingfilm (plastic wrap) and a tea towel (dish cloth) if you prefer. Leave the dough to rest for 30 minutes.

8 Divide the dough into eight 115 g/4 oz portions and share around any leftover dough equally between the portions. Mould round (see pages 16–17). The dough has a sticky texture but is easy to work with when dusted with flour – don't panic! Re-cover and allow to rest for 30 minutes.

9 Meanwhile, heat your griddle or a heavy frying pan (skillet) to a medium-low heat (my cooker has heat options 1–6 and I use 3 for cooking Pumpkin Bake).

10 Roll out a couple of portions to 18 cm/7 in rounds (see pages 18–19). You can use flour as needed here!

11 Place one of the rounds on the preheated, ungreased griddle or pan and bake for 1 minute on each side – use a timer because they shouldn't be overcooked. As the first side cooks, you will see lots of bubbles forming on top. When you turn the bake over, don't mush it down on the griddle – there's no need too. The finished first side will have small brown spots and when you've finished the second side, it will have large brown spots where the bubbles were.

12 Wrap the bake in a tea towel to keep it soft and set it on a cooling rack.

13 As you cook the second round, continue rolling out the remaining portions and carry on cooking and rolling (you really do need that timer!).

14 Serve warm.

Lager Cornbread

Bread made with lager gives it an excellent texture, with that lovely colour from the yellow cornmeal. The fried spring onions just add to the moistness and flavour. This cornbread goes perfectly with chilli con carne or other similar, slightly spicy and strong dishes and is light, crumbly and full of flavour.

MAKES 9 SQUARES

100 g/3½ oz butter

100 g/3½ oz trimmed spring onions (scallions), chopped

100 g/3½ oz plain (all-purpose) flour

100 g/3½ oz wholemeal flour

100 g/3½ oz cornmeal

15 g/½ oz baking powder

5 g/1 tsp salt

30 g/1 oz light muscovado sugar

2 eggs

185 g/6½ oz lager

1 Preheat the oven to 230°C/450°F/gas 8/fan oven 210°C. Grease and flour a 20 cm/8 in square baking tin (pan).

2 In a small frying pan (skillet), melt the butter and add the spring onions. Fry (sauté) over a medium heat for about 4 minutes until softened. Set aside to cool a bit.

3 Sift the flours, cornmeal, baking powder, salt and sugar into a large bowl; you may need to push the sugar through the sieve (strainer) with a spoon. Tip any bits of wholemeal flour left in the sieve into the bowl as well. Stir thoroughly to combine.

4 In a large jug, combine the eggs and the lager and beat together with a fork.

5 When the oven has preheated, pour all the wet ingredients into the dry and stir together thoroughly with a wooden spoon.

6 Pour the batter into the prepared tin. It will seem as though you don't have enough mix but don't worry as the bread will rise a lot.

7 Bake for 15–20 minutes until golden and the sides are pulling away from the sides of the tin. Remove from the oven and rest in the tin for 5 minutes.

8 You can either cut the bread into large squares in the tin (the first piece tends to get mushed up a bit) or turn the whole bread out on to a cooling rack, place another cooling rack on top of the bread and flip the whole thing right side up again. Leave for a few minutes (the cornbread is very crumbly when hot), then cut into large squares.

9 Cornbread is at its best warm and eaten on the same day.

Hushpuppies

Hushpuppies are basically little deep-fried balls of cornbread – and they are gorgeous! Give these a try with your fish and chips; I think you'll like them. Make sure you have the oil at the right temperature when you fry them so that they cook quickly and are light and delicious.

MAKES 8–9 HUSHPUPPIES

70 g/2½ oz cornmeal
150 g/5 oz plain (all-purpose) flour
7.5 g/1½ tsp baking powder
¾ tsp salt
¼ tsp garlic powder
A pinch of cayenne pepper
1 egg, beaten
5 g/1 tsp oil
2 or 3 spring onions (scallions), finely chopped
135 g/4¾ oz milk
Sunflower oil for deep-frying

1 Place all the dry ingredients in a medium-sized bowl and stir thoroughly.

2 Mix together all the wet ingredients in a small bowl.

3 Add the wet ingredients to the dry and mix everything to a paste.

4 Allow the mix to rest for 20 minutes. You could make the hushpuppies straight away but you'd get funny shapes – though that can be fun too.

5 Preheat the deep-fat fryer to 180°C/350°F or until a cube of day-old bread sinks in the oil, then rises to the top and browns in 1 minute.

6 Drop 4 or 5 generous walnut-sized balls off the end of a tablespoon into the hot oil. You may need to loosen them from the bottom of the basket a short time after they go in.

7 Fry (sauté) for 7 minutes, turning them over half way through the cooking time so they are an even dark golden-brown all over.

8 The hushpuppies are ready when the dough is all cooked and they are light yet slightly chewy. Cut one open to test if it is ready, and give the rest a bit longer if necessary.

9 Drain on kitchen paper (paper towels). Keep the finished hushpuppies warm in a low oven while you finish frying the rest.

10 Best eaten straight away.

Almost Instant Doughnuts

I thought, if Hushpuppies work this way (see page 139), then why not doughnuts? I like these; the vanilla really comes through and they are so easy. Most will come out as nice little balls but you will get some funny ones too! These are best eaten straight away, as they get a bit chewy when cold.

MAKES 10 DOUGHNUTS

FOR THE DOUGH
200 g/7 oz plain (all-purpose) flour
10 g/2 tsp dried milk powder (non-fat dry milk)

40 g/1½ oz caster (superfine) sugar
½ tablespoon baking powder
⅛ tsp salt
1 egg, beaten
120 g/4¼ oz milk

5 g/1 tsp oil
5 g/1 tsp vanilla essence (extract)
Sunflower oil for deep-frying

FOR THE TOPPING
Caster sugar or vanilla sugar

1 Place all the dough ingredients in a bowl and beat the mixture with a fork until thoroughly combined and smooth. Set the batter aside to rest for 20 minutes.

2 Preheat the deep-fat fryer or a heavy-based pan of oil to 180°C/350°F or until a cube of day-old bread sinks in the oil, then rises to the top and browns in 1 minute.

3 Give the batter a quick stir. Working in batches and without over-filling the pan, drop walnut-sized balls off the end of a tablespoon into the hot oil and fry (sauté) for 6–7 minutes, turning them occasionally, until they are evenly golden-brown.

4 Remove from the pan with a slotted spoon and drain on kitchen paper (paper towels).

5 Roll the doughnuts in caster or vanilla sugar and serve warm.

Almost Instant Chocolate Doughnuts

These are very chocolatey but not overly sweet and are so easy to make. Unlike Almost Instant Doughnuts (see opposite), this chocolate version stays quite tender when cold so you can eat them straight away or wait a bit – if you can! That's generally a bit of a problem in my house, you won't be surprised to hear.

MAKES 10 DOUGHNUTS

FOR THE DOUGH
160 g/5½ oz plain (all-purpose) flour
40 g/1½ oz cocoa (unsweetened chocolate) powder

10 g/2 tsp dried milk powder (non-fat dry milk)
40 g/1½ oz dark muscovado sugar
½ tablespoon baking powder
⅛ tsp salt
1 egg, beaten

140 g/5 oz milk
5 g/1 tsp oil
5 g/1 tsp vanilla essence (extract)
Sunflower oil for deep-frying
FOR THE TOPPING
Caster (superfine) sugar or vanilla sugar

1   Place all the dough ingredients in a bowl and beat the mixture with a fork until thoroughly combined and smooth. Set the batter aside to rest for 20 minutes.

2   Preheat a deep-fat fryer or a heavy-based pan of oil to 180°C/350°F or until a cube of day-old bread sinks in the oil, then rises to the top and browns in 1 minute.

3   Give the batter a quick stir. Working in batches and without over-filling the pan, drop walnut-sized balls off the end of a tablespoon into the hot oil and fry (sauté) for 6–7 minutes, turning them occasionally, until they are evenly dark brown.

4   Remove from the pan with a slotted spoon and drain on kitchen paper (paper towels).

5   Roll the doughnuts in caster or vanilla sugar and serve warm.

Swirly, Choccy, Nutty Banana Bread

The chocolate and banana breads I had made with cocoa powder just weren't intense enough. Then I was shelling some leftover nuts and I found I only had about half the amount I needed for my normal recipe, so I added melted chocolate to half the batter. Result: intense chocolate and banana with wonderful contrast.

MAKES 1 LOAF

FOR THE DOUGH
115 g/4 oz butter
200 g/7 oz light muscovado sugar
500 g/1 lb 2 oz very ripe bananas
  (unpeeled weight)

2 eggs, lightly beaten
240 g/8¹/₂ oz plain (all-purpose) flour
100 g/3¹/₂ oz wholemeal bread flour
¹/₂ tsp salt
5 g/1 tsp bicarbonate of soda (baking
  soda)
70 g/2¹/₂ oz very hot water

FOR THE FILLING
50 g/1³/₄ oz plain (semi-sweet) chocolate
  with at least 70% cocoa solids
50 g/1³/₄ oz nuts

1   Grease and flour a 900 g/2 lb 23 x 13 cm/ 9 x 5 in loaf tin (pan).

2   Melt the butter in a large bowl over a pan of simmering water or briefly in the microwave. Place the bowl on your work surface and add the sugar. Mix thoroughly.

3   Peel the bananas and mash them with a fork in a medium-sized bowl. Add them to the butter and sugar and mix thoroughly.

4   In the same bowl you used for the bananas, beat the eggs with the fork, then add to the banana mixture.

5   Sift the flours, salt and bicarbonate of soda into another bowl. Add in all the little bits from the wholemeal flour that have stayed in the sieve (strainer).

6   Add the flour mixture and the hot water to the banana mixture in four goes: first add half the flour and mix in thoroughly; then half the water and mix in thoroughly; then the remaining flour; then the remaining water. Mix really thoroughly between each addition.

7   Melt the chocolate in a bowl over a pan of simmering water or briefly in the microwave. Toast the nuts in a preheated oven at 180°C/350°F/gas 4/fan oven 160°C for 6–7 minutes. Reduce the oven temperature to 160°C/325°F/gas 3/fan oven 140°C.

8   Place half the banana bread batter in the bowl you used for the flour. Add the melted chocolate and the chopped nuts to the remaining batter.

9   Add alternate large dollops of the plain and chocolate batters to the prepared tin until you have used up both batters.

10 Using a knife or a skewer and starting at one end of the tin, slowly snake your way from side to side until you reach the other end of the tin to give the banana bread a marbled effect. Once through the tin is enough.

11 Bake in the centre of the preheated oven for 1 hour and 10 minutes or until the loaf is well risen and the edges are pulling away from the sides of the tin.

12 Transfer to a wire rack and cool for 10 minutes in the tin.

13 Tip the loaf out of its tin on to the cooling rack, turn it right side up and allow to cool quite a bit more before slicing – it is very tender!

Poppy Seed and Almond Banana Bread

I love this wonderful bread – and it doesn't even have any chocolate! I wonder why we don't see poppy seeds and almonds together more often, because the combination is incredibly moreish. The lemony tang I've added here just makes it even more delicious. A lovely teatime bread for family and friends.

MAKES 1 LOAF

FOR THE DOUGH
115 g/4 oz butter
110 g/3²/₃ oz light muscovado sugar
100 g/3¹/₂ oz caster (superfine) sugar
500 g/1 lb 2 oz very ripe bananas (unpeeled weight)
2 eggs, lightly beaten

15 g/¹/₂ oz almond essence (extract)
Zest of 1 lemon
240 g/8¹/₂ oz plain (all-purpose) flour
100 g/3¹/₂ oz wholemeal bread flour
¹/₂ tsp salt
5 g/1 tsp bicarbonate of soda (baking soda)
40 g/1¹/₂ oz very hot water
30 g/1 oz lemon juice

FOR THE FILLING
50 g/1³/₄ oz flaked (slivered) almonds
70 g/2¹/₂ oz poppy seeds
FOR THE TOPPING
30 g/1 oz flaked almonds

1 Preheat the oven to 180°C/350°F/gas 4/fan oven 160°C. Grease and flour a 900 g/2 lb 23 x 13 cm/ 9 x 5 in loaf tin (pan).

2 Place the almonds for the filling on a baking (cookie) sheet and toast in the oven for 5–6 minutes. Remove from the oven and set aside. Reduce the oven temperature to 160°C/ 325°F/gas 3/fan oven 140°C.

3 Melt the butter in a large bowl over a pan of simmering water or briefly in the microwave. Place the bowl on your work surface and add the sugars. Mix thoroughly.

4 Peel the bananas and mash them with a fork in a medium-sized bowl. Add them to the butter and sugar and mix thoroughly.

5 In the same bowl you used for the bananas, beat the eggs with the fork, then add to the banana mixture. Add the almond essence and lemon zest.

6 Sift the flours, salt and bicarbonate of soda into another bowl. Add in all the little bits from the

wholemeal flour that have stayed in the sieve (strainer).

7   Mix together the hot water and lemon juice.

8   Add the flour mixture and the hot lemon water to the banana mixture in four goes: first add half the flour and mix in thoroughly; then half the liquid and mix in thoroughly; then the remaining flour; then the remaining liquid. Mix really thoroughly between each addition.

9   Mix in the toasted almonds and the poppy seeds and stir thoroughly.

10   Spoon the batter into the prepared tin and sprinkle the flaked almonds evenly over the top.

11   Bake in the centre of the preheated oven for 1 hour and 10 minutes or until the loaf is well risen and the edges are pulling away from the sides of the tin.

12   Transfer to a wire rack and cool for 10 minutes in the tin. Then tip the loaf out of the tin on to the rack (you may need to loosen it by carefully running a butter knife round the edges) and turn it right side up to finish cooling.

Banana, Rose and Cardamom Loaf

I really like the texture that banana gives to a loaf, and this one has a lovely rich flavour, complemented by the wonderful aromatic cardamom and just a subtle hint of rose water. It cuts well and you can serve it on its own or with a thin spread of fresh butter. You really must give this one a try!

MAKES 1 LOAF

115 g/4 oz butter

200 g/7 oz light muscovado sugar

500 g/1 lb 2 oz very ripe bananas (unpeeled weight)

2 eggs, lightly beaten

40 g/1½ oz rose water

240 g/8½ oz plain (all-purpose) flour

100 g/3½ oz wholemeal flour

½ tsp salt

5 g/1 tsp bicarbonate of soda (baking soda)

10 cardamom pods, split and the seeds ground

70 g/2½ oz very hot water

1 Preheat the oven to 160°C/325°F/gas 3/fan oven 140°C. Grease and flour a 900 g/2 lb 23 x 13 cm/ 9 x 5 in loaf tin (pan).

2 Melt the butter in a large bowl over a pan of simmering water or briefly in the microwave. Place the bowl on your work surface and add the sugar. Mix thoroughly.

3 Peel the bananas and mash them with a fork in a medium-sized bowl. Add them to the butter and sugar and mix thoroughly.

4 In the same bowl you used for the bananas, beat the eggs with the fork, then add to the banana mixture. Add the rose water.

5 Sift the flours, salt, bicarbonate of soda and ground cardamom seeds into another bowl. Add in all the little bits from the wholemeal flour that have stayed in the sieve (strainer).

6 Add the flour mixture and the hot water to the banana mixture in four goes: first add half the flour and mix in thoroughly; then half the water and mix in thoroughly; then the remaining flour; then the remaining water. Mix really thoroughly between each addition.

7 Spoon the batter into the prepared tin and bake in the centre of the preheated oven for 1 hour and 10 minutes or until the loaf is well risen and the edges are pulling away from the sides of the tin.

8 Transfer to a wire rack and cool for 10 minutes in the tin, then tip the loaf out of the tin on to the rack and turn it right side up to finish cooling.

MUFFINS

Muffins are very easy to make, very easy to eat and they can accompany any meal. You combine your dry ingredients; you combine your wet ingredients; then you fold them together with a large metal spoon until the batter is just mixed (never overmix muffins or they'll have flat tops).

At this point you either spoon the batter into a greased or paper-lined muffin tin or gently fold in filling ingredients such as nuts, fruits and seeds. Muffins can also be topped with nuts, crumble, sugar, coconut – just about anything really – or you can leave them plain and enjoy their characteristic crisp top.

Muffins are best eaten warm. They do go stale quickly, but freeze, defrost and reheat very well.

They are not suitable for your breadmaker – but they are so easy to make that it doesn't really matter.

Bacon, Chilli, Peanut Butter and Cornmeal Muffins

This combination may sound a little odd but the saltiness of the bacon works with the sweetness of the peanut butter and the chilli rounds off the flavours with its savoury heat. I use crunchy peanut butter but smooth is also good. Like most muffins, these are best eaten warm and are especially good with butter.

MAKES 9 MUFFINS

50 g/1¾ oz oil
130 g/4½ oz smoked back bacon, chopped

1 large, fat red chilli, chopped
50 g/1¾ oz crunchy peanut butter
200 g/7 oz plain (all-purpose) flour
100 g/3½ oz cornmeal

15 g/½ oz baking powder
30 g/1 oz light muscovado sugar
2 eggs
185 g/6½ oz milk

1. Preheat the oven to 200°C/400°F/gas 6/fan oven 180°C. Grease and flour nine section of a muffin tin (pan) or line with paper liners.

2. Place the oil in a frying pan (skillet) over a medium heat. Add the bacon and chilli and fry (sauté) for about 4 minutes.

3. Add the peanut butter and allow it to melt, then take the pan off the heat and allow it to cool a little.

4. Sift the flour, cornmeal, baking powder and sugar into a large bowl.

5. Beat together the eggs and milk in a jug.

6. Add the contents of the jug along with the contents of the frying pan to the flour mixture. Using a large metal spoon, fold everything together until just combined.

7. Spoon the batter into the muffin tin and bake for 18–20 minutes until the muffins are well risen, golden and the tops spring back when gently pressed with a finger.

8. Transfer to a wire rack to cool a little before eating.

Sweet Potato Muffins

I think these moist and spicy muffins are at their absolute best when eaten warm. Even though these are a sweet muffin, they go really well with sausage, bacon or other savoury flavours as the contrast works so effectively. I do like mixing sweet and savoury! Try them freshly baked for breakfast one day.

MAKES 12 MUFFINS

370 g/13 oz sweet potatoes
200 g/7 oz dark muscovado sugar
100 g/3¹/₂ oz pecans
300 g/10¹/₂ oz plain (all-purpose) flour

15 g/¹/₂ oz baking powder
¹/₂ tsp salt
10 g/2 tsp ground cinnamon
¹/₈ tsp ground cloves
5 g/1 tsp grated nutmeg
¹/₂ tsp ground allspice

100 g/3¹/₂ oz butter, melted
2 eggs
200 g/7 oz milk
5 g/1 tsp vanilla essence (extract)

1   First cook the sweet potatoes. I find this easiest to do according to the microwave instructions for a baked potato. Alternatively, bake them like jacket potatoes in the oven, or you can boil them in their skins until tender, or peel and steam until tender. When the sweet potatoes are cooked, weigh out 250 g/9 oz and use a fork to mash them together with the sugar. Allow the mixture to cool until warm.

2   Preheat the oven to 200°C/400°F/gas 6/fan oven 180°C. Grease and flour 12 sections of a muffin tin (pan) or line with paper liners.

3   Reserve 12 whole pecans for the topping and toast the remainder in the oven for about 6–7 minutes until golden, then chop the toasted nuts.

4   Sift the flour, baking powder, salt, cinnamon, cloves, nutmeg and allspice into a large bowl.

5   Add the melted butter, eggs, milk and vanilla to the sweet potato mixture and mix thoroughly with the fork.

6   Add the sweet potato mixture to the flour mixture and fold together with a large metal spoon until just combined. Carefully fold in the chopped nuts.

7   Spoon the batter into the muffin tin and press a whole nut on top of each muffin.

8   Bake for 20–22 minutes until the muffins are well risen and the tops spring back when you press them gently.

9   Transfer to a wire rack to cool a little before eating.

If You Need Chocolate Muffins

I love deep, dark, intense chocolate and I like it warm and melting – you may have worked that out by now if you've made any of my earlier recipes! These muffins satisfy all my desires, are irresistible and way too easy to make. Try to give them a few moments cooling on the rack, then devour. Why fight it?

MAKES 12 MUFFINS

FOR THE BATTER
115 g/4 oz butter
100 g/3½ oz plain (semi-sweet) chocolate with at least 70% cocoa solids

280 g/10 oz plain (all-purpose) flour
200 g/7 oz light muscovado sugar
5 g/1 tsp bicarbonate of soda (baking soda)
⅛ tsp salt
1 egg, beaten

100 g/3½ oz plain yoghurt
150 g/5 oz milk
10 g/2 tsp vanilla essence (extract)
FOR THE FILLING
150 g/5 oz plain chocolate, chopped into rough chunks

1 Preheat the oven to 190°C/375°F/gas 5/fan oven 170°C. Grease and flour 12 sections of a muffin tin (pan) or line with paper liners.

2 Melt the butter and chocolate in a bowl over a saucepan of water on a low heat. Remove from the heat.

3 Sift the flour, sugar, baking soda and salt into a large bowl. You may need to push the sugar through the sieve with a spoon.

4 Whisk together the egg, yoghurt, milk and vanilla in a separate bowl. Stir into the chocolate and butter.

5 Fold the chocolate mixture into the flour with a large metal spoon until just blended, then fold in the chocolate chunks.

6 Divide the mixture between the muffin tin. Lick the spoon and the bowl!

7 Bake for 22–25 minutes until the muffins are risen and spring back when you gently press them – watch out for hot, melted chocolate chunks!

8 Transfer to a wire rack to cool a little before eating.

Cocoa, Coconut and Chocolate Chunk Muffins

These chocolate muffins are full of sweet coconut, melting chunks of white and dark chocolate – and a shot of Malibu to give them a real kick! If you can call a muffin handsome – and I would argue that you can – then I think these qualify. A very adult treat, and don't we all need one from time to time!

MAKES 12 MUFFINS

FOR THE BATTER
280 g/10 oz plain (all-purpose) flour
30 g/1 oz cocoa (unsweetened chocolate) powder
15 g/1/2 oz baking powder
170 g/6 oz caster (superfine) sugar
1/2 tsp salt
50 g/13/4 oz sweetened desiccated (shredded) coconut
2 eggs
160 g/51/2 oz coconut milk
100 g/31/2 oz oil
40 g/11/2 oz Malibu

FOR THE FILLING
100 g/31/2 oz plain (semi-sweet) chocolate with at least 70 per cent cocoa solids, chopped into rough chunks
100 g/31/2 oz white chocolate, chopped into rough chunks

FOR THE TOPPING
50 g/13/4 oz sweetened desiccated (shredded) coconut

1   Preheat the oven to 200°C/400°F/gas 6/fan oven 180°C. Grease and flour 12 sections of a muffin tin (pan) or line with paper liners.

2   Sift the flour, cocoa, baking powder, sugar and salt into a large bowl. Stir in the desiccated coconut.

3   Combine the eggs, coconut milk, oil and Malibu in a jug or bowl and mix with a fork.

4   Add the contents of the jug or bowl to the flour mixture and fold together with a large metal spoon until just combined. Carefully fold in the chocolate chunks.

5   Spoon into the muffin tin, then sprinkle the coconut topping evenly over each muffin.

6   Bake for 22–24 minutes until the muffins are well risen and the tops spring back when gently pressed with a finger.

7   Transfer to a wire rack to cool a little before eating.

Banana, Chocolate and Peanut Butter Muffins

You know that I enthusiastic about all my recipes, but my first bite of this muffin quite literally made me gasp 'Oh my goodness!' – and promptly shovel in more! Delicious doesn't even come near to describing them, although they are very filling so you'll have to share this batch. Whether you choose smooth or crunchy peanut butter is up to you.

MAKES 7 MUFFINS

FOR THE BATTER
50 g/1¾ oz plain (semi-sweet) chocolate with at least 70 per cent cocoa solids
50 g/1¾ oz peanut butter
60 g/2 oz butter
100 g/3½ oz light muscovado sugar

250 g/9 oz very ripe bananas (unpeeled weight)
1 egg, lightly beaten
½ tsp vanilla essence (extract)
100 g/3½ oz plain (all-purpose) flour
50 g/1¾ oz wholemeal flour
¼ tsp salt

½ tsp bicarbonate of soda (baking soda)
35 g/generous 1 oz very hot water
FOR THE FILLING
50 g/1¾ oz plain chocolate with at least 70% cocoa solids, chopped into chunks
7 tsp peanut butter

1 Melt the chocolate and peanut butter together in a small bowl over a pan of simmering water. Remove from the heat.

2 Preheat the oven to 160°C/325°F/gas 3/fan oven 145°C. Grease and flour 7 sections of a muffin tin (pan) or line with paper liners.

3 Melt the butter in a large bowl over a pan of simmering water or briefly in the microwave. Add the sugar and mix thoroughly.

4 Peel the bananas and mash in a medium-sized bowl. Add to the butter and sugar and mix thoroughly.

5 In the same bowl you used for the bananas, beat the egg with the fork. Add the egg to the banana mixture and stir in the vanilla.

6 Sift the flours, salt and bicarbonate of soda into a separate bowl. Tip in all the little bits from the wholemeal flour that stayed in the sieve (strainer).

7 Add half the flour to the banana mixture and mix it in thoroughly. Then add the hot water and mix it in thoroughly. Then add the rest of the flour and stir thoroughly. Stir in the melted chocolate and peanut butter and mix it in thoroughly. Stir in the chocolate chunks.

8 Spoon just a little of the muffin batter into each prepared section of the muffin tin, not even half filling it. Add a teaspoonful of peanut butter to the centre of each. Cover the peanut butter with the remaining batter, filling the tins evenly.

9 Bake for 30–33 minutes until the muffins are well risen and spring back when you gently press the tops.

10 Transfer to a wire rack to cool.

Milk Chocolate Chunk Muffins

I surprised myself when I created these muffins. I love deep, dark chocolate, but I gave some milk chocolate a try in these muffins and I really enjoyed them. It just goes to show you should try new things sometimes! To my mind they taste a bit like American chocolate chip cookies but obviously with a soft, muffin texture.

MAKES 11 MUFFINS

FOR THE BATTER
400 g/14 oz plain (all-purpose) flour
15 g/¹⁄₂ oz baking powder

¹⁄₈ tsp salt
170 g/6 oz light muscovado sugar
100 g/3¹⁄₂ oz butter
185 g/6¹⁄₂ oz milk
2 eggs

5 g/1 tsp vanilla essence (extract)
FOR THE FILLING
150 g/5 oz milk (sweet) chocolate,
    chopped into chunks

1   Preheat the oven to 180°C/350°F/gas 4/fan oven 160°C. Grease and flour 11 sections of a muffin tin (pan) or line with paper liners.

2   Sift the dry ingredients into a large bowl and stir thoroughly. You will probably have to push some of the sugar through the sieve (strainer) with a wooden spoon.

3   Melt the butter in a small bowl. In another small bowl or a jug, beat together the milk, eggs and vanilla with a fork.

4   Add the wet ingredients to the dry and gently fold together with a large metal spoon until just moistened. Gently fold in the chocolate chunks with the metal spoon.

5   Spoon the batter into the muffin tin.

6   Bake for about 22–25 minutes until the muffins are well risen and golden. The tops of the muffins will spring back when you gently press on them.

7   Transfer to a wire rack to cool.

White Chocolate and Lavender Muffins

Romantic and yummy! You could use just granulated sugar for the topping but lavender sugar gives it a wonderful subtle flavour and is so easy to make. Just put a few sprigs of lavender in a jar of sugar, put on the lid and leave it for a few hours or overnight. An unusual and delightful variety to add to the repertoire of chocolate muffins.

MAKES 11 MUFFINS

FOR THE BATTER
370 g/13 oz plain (all-purpose) flour
170 g/6 oz caster (superfine) sugar
15 g/½ oz baking powder

⅛ tsp salt
1 tbsp fresh lavender florets
   or 1 tsp dried
185 g/6½ oz milk
100 g/3½ oz oil
2 eggs

FOR THE FILLING
200 g/7 oz white chocolate, chopped
FOR THE TOPPING
40 g/1½ oz lavender sugar

1   Preheat the oven to 180°C/350°F/gas 4/fan oven 160°C. Grease and flour 11 sections of a muffin tin or line with paper liners.

2   Sift all the dry ingredients except the lavender into a large bowl. Stir in the lavender.

3   Combine the remaining dough ingredients in a small bowl or jug and beat thoroughly with a fork.

4   Add the wet ingredients to the dry and fold together with a large metal spoon until just moistened. Very gently fold in the white chocolate chunks.

5   Spoon into the muffin tin and sprinkle lavender sugar evenly over the tops.

6   Bake for 22–25 minutes until well risen and golden and the tops spring back when you gently press them.

7   Transfer to a wire rack to cool.

Coffee and Cream Muffins

These sophisticated muffins smell wonderful when they are just baked – an utterly irresistible aroma – so you won't find they hang around on the plate for long. Try baking them if you are trying to sell your house! The double cream gives their texture a luscious softness that everyone will love. Coffee heaven!

MAKES 11 MUFFINS

FOR THE BATTER
300 g/10½ oz plain (all-purpose) flour
170 g/6 oz caster (superfine) sugar

15 g/½ oz baking powder
30 g/1 oz instant coffee granules
⅛ tsp salt
100 g/3½ oz milk
185 g/6½ oz double (heavy) cream

100 g/3½ oz oil
2 eggs
FOR THE TOPPING
40 g/1½ oz demerara sugar

1   Preheat the oven to 180°C/350°F/gas 4/fan oven 160°C. Grease and flour 11 sections of a muffin tin (pan) or line with paper liners.

2   Sift the dry ingredients into a large bowl. You may need to push the coffee thorough the sieve (strainer) with the back of a spoon.

3   Combine the wet ingredients in a small bowl and mix together with a fork but try not to thicken the cream.

4   Add the wet ingredients to dry and gently fold together with a large metal spoon until just moistened.

5   Spoon into the prepared muffin tin about three-quarters full and sprinkle the tops with the demerara sugar.

6   Bake for about 23–25 minutes until well risen and the tops spring back when you gently press on them.

7   Transfer to a wire rack to cool.

Christmas Muffins

Imagine inhaling the heady scent of Grand Marnier, savouring the delicate crunch of almonds and demerara sugar, feeling the jewel-like red cranberries bursting in your mouth and enjoying melting, white chocolate! For extra luxury, I dust the tops of the baked muffins with gold cake-decorating powder. Merry Christmas!

MAKES 12 MUFFINS

FOR THE BATTER
310 g/11 oz plain (all-purpose) flour
170 g/6 oz caster (superfine) sugar
15 g/¹/₂ oz baking powder
¹/₈ tsp salt
50 g/1³/₄ oz ground almonds

100 g/3¹/₂ oz Grand Marnier
100 g/3¹/₂ oz milk
100 g/3¹/₂ oz oil
5 g/1 tsp almond essence (extract)
2 eggs

FOR THE FILLING
200 g/7 oz fresh or frozen cranberries (you can use them straight from the freezer)
150 g/5 oz white chocolate, chopped

FOR THE TOPPING
40 g/1¹/₂ oz flaked (slivered) almonds
30 g/1 oz demerara sugar
Gold dusting powder (optional)

1. Preheat the oven to 200°C/400°F/gas 6/fan oven 180°C. Grease and flour 12 sections of a muffin tin (pan) or line with paper liners.

2. Sift the flour, sugar, baking powder and salt into a large bowl. Stir in the ground almonds.

3. Combine the wet ingredients in small bowl or a jug and mix thoroughly with a fork.

4. Add the wet ingredients to the dry and fold together with a large metal spoon until just moistened. Very gently fold in the cranberries and chocolate.

5. Spoon into the prepared muffin tin and sprinkle evenly with the flaked almonds and demerara sugar.

6. Bake for 22–25 minutes until the muffins are well risen and golden. The tops will spring back when gently pressed.

7. Transfer to a wire rack. Decorate the almond topping with gold dusting powder if you wish and serve warm.

Clementine and Clove Muffins

These make a mouth-watering, not-too-sweet Christmas muffin. But you don't have to wait until Christmas: you can enjoy them any time of year. They are full of flavour and smell wonderful too! They are surprising good with cheese as the sweet and savoury flavours complement each other really well.

MAKES 10 MUFFINS

FOR THE BATTER
200 g/7 oz plain (all-purpose) flour
100 g/3¹/₂ oz wholemeal bread flour
15 g/¹/₂ oz baking powder

¹/₈ tsp salt
¹/₂ tsp ground cloves
40 g/1¹/₂ oz ground almonds
Grated zest and juice of 3 clementines
A little milk
2 eggs

5 g/1 tsp almond essence (extract)
100 g/3¹/₂ oz butter
170 g/6 oz dark muscovado sugar
FOR THE TOPPING
40 g/1¹/₂ oz demerara sugar
Gold dusting powder (optional)

1   Preheat the oven to 200°C/400°F/gas 6/fan oven 180°C. Grease and flour 10 sections of a muffin tin (pan) or line with paper liners.

2   Sift the flours, baking powder, salt and cloves into a large bowl. Tip in all the little bits from the wholemeal flour that stayed in the sieve (strainer). Stir in the ground almonds and the clementine zest.

3   Make up the clementine juice to 170 g/6 oz with milk. Combine with the eggs and almond essence in small bowl or a jug and mix thoroughly.

4   Melt the butter in a bowl over a pan of simmering water or briefly in the microwave. Place the bowl on your work surface and add the muscovado sugar. Stir thoroughly.

5   Add the wet ingredients to the dry and fold together with a large metal spoon until just moistened.

6   Spoon into the prepared muffin tin and sprinkle evenly with the demerara sugar.

7   Bake for 20–22 minutes until the muffins are well risen and golden. The tops will spring back when gently pressed.

8   Transfer to a wire rack. Decorate the tops with gold dusting powder if you wish and serve warm.

Poppy Seed and Almond Muffins

This recipe makes delicious light muffins, which still have the lovely rich flavour of the ground almonds, with just a touch of citrus from the lemon to give them a bit of zest. They look beautiful, too, speckled with the poppy seeds across the lovely lemon centre. Just look at that photograph. Doesn't it make you want to get baking?

MAKES 10 MUFFINS

FOR THE BATTER
310 g/11 oz plain (all-purpose) flour
170 g/6 oz caster (superfine) sugar
15 g/¹⁄₂ oz baking powder

¹⁄₈ tsp salt
50 g/1³⁄₄ oz ground almonds
40 g/1¹⁄₂ oz poppy seeds
Grated zest and juice of 1 lemon
A little milk
2 eggs

5 g/1 tsp almond essence (extract)
100 g/3¹⁄₂ oz butter
FOR THE TOPPING
50 g/1³⁄₄ oz flaked (slivered) almonds

1 Preheat the oven to 180°C/350°F/gas 4/fan oven 160°C. Grease and flour 10 section of a muffin tin (pan) or line with paper liners.

2 Sift the flour, sugar, baking powder and salt into a large bowl. Stir in the ground almonds, poppy seeds and lemon zest.

3 Make up the lemon juice to 170 g/6 oz with milk. Combine with the eggs and almond essence in a small bowl or a jug. Beat together thoroughly with a fork.

4 Melt the butter in a saucepan, in a bowl over a pan of simmering water, or briefly in the microwave.

5 Add the contents of the jug or small bowl and the melted butter to the dry ingredients and fold together with a large metal spoon until just combined.

6 Divide the batter between the muffin tins and sprinkle evenly with the flaked almonds.

7 Bake for 23–25 minutes until golden, well risen and the muffins spring back when lightly pressed.

8 Transfer to a wire rack to cool a little before eating.

Pistachio, Anise and Almond Muffins

The development of this muffin recipe was inspired by eating cantucci biscuits. They are traditional almond and honey biscuits from Tuscany in Italy, which are made to be dipped in Vin Santo, a sweet, golden dessert wine with a full-bodied and light flavour and a slightly penetrating aroma.

MAKES 12 MUFFINS

FOR THE BATTER
1 tbsp anise seeds
$\frac{1}{8}$ tsp salt
310 g/11 oz plain (all-purpose) flour

170 g/6 oz caster (superfine) sugar
15 g/$\frac{1}{2}$ oz baking powder
60 g/2 oz ground almonds
170 g/6 oz milk
2 eggs
5 g/1 tsp almond essence (extract)

100 g/3$\frac{1}{2}$ oz butter
FOR THE FILLING AND TOPPING
100 g/3$\frac{1}{2}$ oz whole almonds
100 g/3$\frac{1}{2}$ oz pistachio nuts, roughly chopped
30 g/1 oz demerara sugar

1 Preheat the oven to 180°C/350°F/gas 4/fan oven 160°C. Grease and flour 12 sections of a muffin tin (pan) or line with paper liners.

2 Grind the anise with the salt using a pestle and mortar. Place the whole almonds on a baking (cookie) sheet and toast in the preheated oven for 7–8 minutes. Roughly chop the almonds.

3 Sift the flour, sugar and baking powder into a large bowl. Stir in the ground anise and the ground almonds.

4 Combine the milk, eggs and almond essence in a small bowl or a jug. Beat together thoroughly with a fork.

5 Melt the butter in a saucepan, in a bowl over a pan of simmering water, or briefly in the microwave.

6 Add the contents of the small bowl or jug and the melted butter to the dry ingredients and fold together with a metal spoon until just combined. Fold in 70 g/2$\frac{1}{2}$ oz each of the toasted almonds and the pistachios. Chop the remaining nuts even finer.

7 Divide the batter evenly between the muffin tins.

8 Mix the remaining chopped nuts with the demerara sugar and sprinkle evenly over the muffins.

9 Bake for 22–25 minutes until well risen and the muffins spring back when lightly pressed.

10 Transfer to a wire rack and allow to cool a little before eating.

Sweet Cornmeal and Peanut Crumble Muffins

Unusual but very tasty, these definitely have an American feel to them. You can buy cornmeal in most large supermarkets now, though they sometimes call it polenta, in which case you'll find it with the Italian-style ingredients. It has a lovely pale yellow colour and a distinctive texture that just goes so well with the peanut crumble topping.

MAKES 12 MUFFINS

100 g/3½ oz light muscovado sugar
100 g/3½ oz unsalted butter
90 g/3 oz honey
160 g/5½ oz milk
2 eggs

FOR THE TOPPING
50 g/1¾ oz unsalted butter, softened
80 g/2¾ oz plain flour
30 g/1 oz cornmeal
20 g/¾ oz honey
20 g/¾ oz light muscovado sugar
50 g/1¾ oz raw peanuts

FOR THE BATTER
200 g/7 oz plain (all-purpose) flour
100 g/3½ oz cornmeal
15 g/½ oz baking powder
⅛ tsp salt

1 Preheat the oven to 180°C/350°F/gas 4/fan oven 160°C. Grease and flour 12 sections of a muffin tin or line with paper liner. Place the peanuts for the topping on a baking (cookie) sheet and toast in the preheated oven for 10 minutes. Roughly chop the peanuts.

2 Sift the dry dough ingredients into a large bowl. You may need to push the sugar through the sieve (strainer) with a wooden spoon.

3 Melt the butter in a saucepan, in a bowl over a pan of simmering water, or briefly in the microwave. Add the honey, mix together and set aside.

4 Combine the milk and eggs in a small bowl and beat together with a fork.

5 Add the wet ingredients to the dry and gently fold together with a large metal spoon until just moistened. The batter may look a bit thin at first but the cornmeal is very absorbent.

6 Spoon the batter into the muffin tin, a little less than three-quarters full.

7 Combine and rub together the topping ingredients in a small bowl. Sprinkle evenly over the muffins.

8 Bake for 20–22 minutes until well risen and golden and the tops of the muffins spring back when gently pressed.

9 Transfer to wire rack to cool a little before eating.

Pineapple, Blueberry and Coconut Muffins

These are lovely fruity muffins with plenty of coconut flavour and a splendid texture.
You will need to drain the can of pineapple pieces very thoroughly – really press the juice
out of the fruit using the lid. This should leave you with 160 g/5¹/₂ oz of pineapple pieces for
the recipe.

MAKES 12 MUFFINS

FOR THE BATTER
310 g/11 oz plain (all-purpose) flour
170 g/6 oz caster (superfine) sugar
15 g/¹/₂ oz baking powder
¹/₈ tsp salt

50 g/1³/₄ oz sweetened desiccated
   (shredded) coconut
100 g/3¹/₂ oz Malibu
100 g/3¹/₂ oz coconut milk
100 g/3¹/₂ oz oil
2 eggs

FOR THE FILLING
227 g/8 oz/1 small can of pineapple pieces
   in juice, drained
125 g/4¹/₃ oz blueberries

FOR THE TOPPING
50 g/1³/₄ oz sweetened desiccated
   (shredded) coconut

1 Preheat the oven to 200°C/400°F/gas 6/fan oven 180°C. Grease and flour 12 sections of a muffin tin or line with paper liners.

2 Sift dry ingredients except the coconut into a large bowl. Stir in the coconut.

3 Combine the wet ingredients in small bowl or a jug.

4 Add the wet ingredients to the dry and fold together with a large metal spoon until just moistened.

5 Very gently fold in the pineapple pieces and the blueberries.

6 Spoon into the muffin tin and sprinkle evenly with the coconut.

7 Bake for 22–25 minutes until the muffins are well risen, golden and the coconut is toasted. The tops will spring back when gently pressed.

8 Transfer to wire rack to cool a little before eating.

Blackberry, Almond and Coconut Muffins

I really like these muffins. They came about one day when we had collected some fat blackberries while out for a walk. I was going to make a simple muffin mix with them but I looked in the cupboard and saw bits and pieces that needed using up, and that's how this combination came together.

MAKES 12 MUFFINS

FOR THE BATTER
320 g/11¼ oz plain (all-purpose) flour
15 g/½ oz baking powder
⅛ tsp salt
170 g/6 oz caster (superfine) sugar

60 g/2 oz ground almonds
20 g/¾ oz sweetened desiccated (shredded) coconut
½ tsp almond essence (extract)
100 g/3½ oz oil
200 g/7 oz milk
2 eggs

FOR THE FILLING
170 g/6 oz fresh or frozen blackberries (you can use them straight from the freezer)

FOR THE TOPPING
40 g/1½ oz flaked (slivered) almonds
40 g/1½ oz sweetened desiccated coconut

1   Preheat the oven to 200°C/400°F/gas 6/fan oven 180°C. Grease and flour 12 sections of a muffin tin or line with paper liners.

2   Sift the dry ingredients into a large bowl. Add the ground almonds and coconut and mix thoroughly.

3   Combine the wet ingredients in a small bowl or a jug and beat thoroughly with a fork.

4   Add the wet ingredients to the dry and fold together with a large metal spoon until just combined. Fold in the blackberries.

5   Divide the batter evenly between the muffin tin.

6   Sprinkle the flaked almonds, then the coconut, evenly on the muffins.

7   Bake for 25–28 minutes until golden, well risen and the muffins spring back when lightly pressed.

8   Transfer to a wire rack to cool a little before eating.

Rhubarb and Strawberry Muffins

These muffins are based on one of our favourite pies. They are full of fruit and very moist, with the lovely green-and-pink rhubarb complemented by the red strawberries and golden cake mix. I like to use muscovado sugar and just a hint of ginger to round out the flavour, too.

MAKES 12 MUFFINS

FOR THE BATTER
300 g/10½ oz plain (all-purpose) flour
15 g/½ oz baking powder
¼ tsp salt

¼ tsp ground ginger
185 g/6½ oz light muscovado sugar
100 g/3½ oz butter
2 eggs
185 g/6½ oz milk
5 g/1 tsp vanilla essence (extract)

FOR THE FILLING
30 g/1 oz sultanas (golden raisins)
100 g/3½ oz rhubarb, chopped
200 g/7 oz strawberries, chopped
FOR THE TOPPING
40 g/1½ oz demerara sugar

1 Preheat the oven to 200°C/400°F/gas 6/fan oven 180°C. Grease and flour 12 sections of a muffin tin or line with paper liners.

2 Sift the dry ingredients into a large bowl. You will need to push the sugar through the sieve (strainer) with the back of a spoon.

3 Melt the butter in a saucepan, in a bowl over a pan of simmering water, or briefly in the microwave.

4 Combine the eggs, milk and vanilla in a small bowl.

5 Add both bowls of wet ingredients to the dry and stir with a large metal spoon until just combined.

6 Combine the filling ingredients in a bowl, then gently fold into the batter. Be careful not to over-stir the batter.

7 Spoon the batter into the prepared muffin tin and sprinkle evenly with the sugar.

8 Bake for 25–27 minutes until well risen and golden and the muffins spring back when lightly pressed.

9 Transfer to a wire rack to cool a little before eating.

Banana, Date and Muesli Crumble Muffins

These are just downright yummy and completely irresistible! You can see in the photograph the wonderful textures created by the coconut, dates and the seeds on the top. You can vary the seeds you use if you don't have these in the storecupboard. I'm sure you'll be experimenting with your own recipes by now.

MAKES 8

FOR THE BATTER
60 g/2 oz butter
100 g/3½ oz light muscovado sugar
250 g/9 oz very ripe bananas (unpeeled weight)
1 egg, lightly beaten
½ tsp vanilla essence (extract)
60 g/2 oz plain (all-purpose) flour

50 g/1¾ oz wholemeal flour
½ tsp bicarbonate of soda (baking soda)
¼ tsp salt
60 g/2 oz porridge oats
35 g/1¼ oz very hot water
FOR THE FILLING
70 g/2½ oz sugar-rolled or ready-to-eat dates, chopped
30 g/1 oz sweetened desiccated (shredded) coconut

FOR THE TOPPING
50 g/1¾ oz jumbo oats
50 g/1¾ oz plain flour
10 g/2 tsp sunflower seeds
5 g/1 tsp sesame seeds
15 g/½ oz light muscovado sugar
20 g/¾ oz honey
25 g/1 oz butter, softened

1. Preheat the oven to 180°C/350°F/gas 4/fan oven 160°C. Grease and flour 8 sections of a muffin tin or line with paper liners.

2. Melt the butter in a large bowl over a pan of simmering water or briefly in the microwave. Place the bowl on your work surface and add the sugar. Mix thoroughly.

3. Peel the bananas and mash them in a medium-sized bowl with a fork. Add them to the butter and sugar and mix thoroughly.

4. In the same bowl you used for the bananas, beat the egg with the fork. Add to the butter mixture, then stir the vanilla.

5. Sift the flours, bicarbonate of soda and salt into a medium-sized bowl. Tip in all the little bits from the wholemeal flour that stayed in the sieve (strainer). Stir in the porridge oats.

6. Add half the flour mixture to the butter mixture and mix it in thoroughly. Add the hot water and mix it in thoroughly. Finally, mix in the remaining flour mixture.

7. Add the filling ingredients and stir thoroughly to combine.

8. Spoon the batter into the muffin tin.

9. Combine and rub together the topping ingredients in a small bowl. Sprinkle evenly over the muffins.

10. Bake for 30–33 minutes or until the muffins are well risen and spring back when you gently press the tops.

11. Transfer to a wire rack to cool a little before eating.

Bibliography

Horn, Jane (ed). *Cooking A to Z California Culinary Academy*. Ortho Books, Robert J Dolezal, 1988.

Humphries, Carolyn. *Real Food: Gluten-free Bread & Cakes from your Breadmaker*. W. Foulsham & Co. Ltd, 2004.

Indar, Polly B, Ramesar, Dorothy B and Bissessar, Sylvia (eds). *Naparima Girl's High School*. Naparima Girls' High School, 1988.

Palmer, Carol. *Real Food: Recipes for Your Breadmaker*. W. Foulsham & Co. Ltd, 2002.

Rhodes, Gary. *Gary Rhodes New British Classics*. BBC Worldwide Ltd, 1999.

Sheasby, Anne. *Light and Lean Cuisine: More Than 200 Simple and Delicious Recipes*. Christine McFadden, Clb, 1998.

Slater, Nigel. *Nigel Slater's Real Food*. Fourth Estate 1999.

Sunset Breads Step-By-Step Techniques. Sunset Books and Sunset Magazine, Lane Publishing Company, 1989.

Treuille, Eric and Ferrigno, Ursula. *Ultimate Bread*. DK Publishing, 1998.

Walden, Hilaire. *The Great Big Cookie Book*. Lorenze Books, 1998.

Index

almonds
  blackberry, almond and coconut
    muffins 162
  pistachio, anise and almond
    muffins 159
  poppy seed and almond banana
    bread 144–145
  poppy seed and almond muffins 158
apple and anise crinkle buns 90–91

bacon
  bacon and Cheddar pizza 112–113
  bacon and marmalade sandwich
    loaf 44–45
  bacon, chilli, peanut butter and
    cornmeal muffins 148
  bacon, egg and maple syrup sandwich
    loaf 55–56
  hot new Mexico buns 86–87
  maple cured bacon pizza 114
bagels 70–71
  cinnamon and raisin bagels 72–73
'bake' 134–135
baking powder 9
bananas
  banana, chocolate and peanut butter
    muffins 152
  banana, chocolate and peanut butter
    sandwich loaf 54–55
  banana, date and muesli crumble
    muffins 164
  banana, rose and cardamom loaf 146
  poppy seed and almond banana
    bread 144–145
  swirly, choccy, nutty banana
    bread 142–143
bialys 74–75
bicarbonate of soda 9
black pepper 9
blackberry, almond and coconut
  muffins 162

bread makers 24–25
buns see bagels; hot crossed buns; rolls
  and buns
butter 9

cardamom
  banana, rose and cardamom loaf 146
cheese
  Christmas Eve pizza 118–119
  hot and spicy mango chutney and
    cheese sandwich loaf 50–51
  wholemeal cheese and onion
    sandwich loaf 48–49
chicken pizza 116
chocolate 9
  almost instant chocolate
    doughnuts 141
  banana, chocolate and peanut butter
    muffins 152
  banana, chocolate and peanut butter
    sandwich loaf 54–55
  chocolate bars 110
  chocolate chip and marshmallow flat
    bread 130–131
  chocolate, coconut and marshmallow
    dunking buns 102–103
  cocoa, coconut and chocolate chunk
    muffins 151
  if you need chocolate muffins 150
  milk chocolate chunk muffins 153
  swirly, choccy, nutty banana
    bread 142–143
  toasted hazelnut and Nutella flat
    bread 124–125
  white chocolate and lavender
    muffins 154
Christmas Eve pizza 118–119
Christmas muffins 156
cinnamon, chocolate and marshmallow
  dunking buns 100–101
Clementine and clove muffins 157

coffee and cream muffins 155
condensed milk dunking buns 104–105
cornmeal
  bacon, chilli, peanut butter and
    cornmeal muffins 148
  corn rows 41
  hushpuppies 139
  lager cornbread 138
  sweet cornmeal and peanut crumble
    muffins 160

deep fried breads
  almost instant chocolate
    doughnuts 141
  almost instant doughnuts 140
  hushpuppies 139
double knots 68–69
dough
  chopping ingredients into 23
  hooks 7, 10
  kneading 7, 12–13
  knocking back 14
  mixing 7, 12–13
  moulding into a head 14
  moulding round 16–17
  problem solving 15, 17
  rising and resting 15
  rolling out 18–22
  texture 12–13
doughnuts
  almost instant chocolate
    doughnuts 141
  almost instant doughnuts 140
dried fruit 9, 23
dunking buns 100–105

eggs 10
equipment 8, 10
  see also bread makers; mixers

fancy bakes 133–146

fancy loaves 57–66
flat breads 121–132
   'bake' 134–135
   pumpkin bake 136–137
flour 10
fruit
   inspired rhubarb, apple and sultana
      bread 62–63

ginger, ginger, gingerbread 58–59
granary loaves
   butter-scented soft granary round 32

Halloween pumpkin bread 38–39
herbs
   yoghurt and herb flat bread 132
hot crossed buns
   chocolate hot crossed buns 80–81
   hot crossed buns 78–79
hot dog sandwich loaf with mustard and
   ketchup 46–47
hushpuppies 139

ingredients 9–10, 11, 12
   chopping into dough 23
   weighing 11, 12

jams 10

kneading 7, 12–13
knives 10
knocking back 14

lager cornbread 138
lavender
   white chocolate and lavender
      muffins 154
liquorice buns 94–95

marmalades 10
marzipan bars 98–99
measuring ingredients 11, 12
mixers 7, 10, 12–13
mixing 7, 12–13

moulding dough
   into a head 14
   moulding round 16–17
muesli
   banana, date and muesli crumble
      muffins 164
   German-inspired muesli rolls 76–77
muffins 147–164

nuts
   buttery, honey and nut loaf 60–61
   sweet cornmeal and peanut crumble
      muffins 160
   swirly, choccy, nutty banana
      bread 142–143
   toasted hazelnut and Nutella flat
      bread 124–125
   see also peanut butter

oats and oatmeal
   toasted golden oat swirls 106–107
   wholemeal and oatmeal loaf 33
oils 10
   olive oil wells 40
olive oil wells 40
ovens 26

parsnip, honey and brown sugar bread 66
pastry scrapers 10
peanut butter
   bacon, chilli, peanut butter and
      cornmeal muffins 148
   banana, chocolate and peanut butter
      muffins 152
   banana, chocolate and peanut butter
      sandwich loaf 54–55
   crunchy peanut butter flat
      bread 122–123
   peanut butter and birdseed
      swirls 108–109
   peanut butter, honey and
      marshmallow sandwich loaf 52–53
pineapple, blueberry and coconut
   muffins 161

pistachio, anise and almond muffins 159
pizza 111–120
   rumpled pizza 88–89
plaited loaves
   beautiful white plait 28–29
poppy seeds
   poppy seed and almond banana
      bread 144–145
   poppy seed and almond muffins 158
potato pizza 117
pumpkins
   Halloween pumpkin bread 38–39
   pumpkin bake 136–137

raisins
   rum and raisin choppy loaf 64–65
resting dough 15
rhubarb
   inspired rhubarb, apple and sultana
      bread 62–63
   rhubarb and strawberry muffins 163
rising dough 15
rolling out 18–22
rolls and buns 67–82
   bialys 74–75
   double knots 68–69
   dunking buns 100–105
   German-inspired muesli rolls 76–77
   lightly spiced wholemeal honey
      coils 82
   sesame squares 42
   see also bagels; hot crossed buns
rolls and buns, filled 83–110
round loaves
   butter-scented soft brown round 31
   butter-scented soft granary round 32
   butter-scented soft white round 30
rum and raisin choppy loaf 64–65
rye
   Tropical wholemeal and rye loaf 34–35
   wholemeal, seeds and rye loaf 36–37

salt 10
sandwich loaves 43–56

sausage pizza 115
scales 10, 11
seafood pizza 120
seeds
    Halloween pumpkin bread 38–39
    peanut butter and birdseed
        swirls 108–109
    poppy seed and almond banana
        bread 144–145
    poppy seed and almond muffins 158
    pumpkin seed flat bread 128–129
    sesame squares 42
    sunflower honey buns 96–97
    wholemeal, seeds and rye loaf 36–37
sesame squares 42

strawberries
    Corin's oaty strawberry pots 92–93
    rhubarb and strawberry muffins 163
sugar 10
sunflower honey buns 96–97
sweet potato muffins 149

tahini flat bread 126–127
temperature 7, 10, 12
Tropical wholemeal and rye loaf 34–35
tuna
    HTBs 84–85

vanilla essence 10

white loaves
    beautiful white plait 28–29
    butter-scented soft white round 30
wholemeal loaves
    butter-scented soft brown round 31
    tropical wholemeal and rye
        loaf 34–35
    wholemeal and oatmeal loaf 33
    wholemeal cheese and onion
        sandwich loaf 48–49
    wholemeal, seeds and rye loaf 36–37

yeast 8, 10, 12, 25
yoghurt and herb flat bread 132